The
Paradox of Cause
and Other Essays

The
Paradox of Cause
and
Other Essays

John William Miller

W · W · Norton & Company
NEW YORK · LONDON

Library of Congress Cataloging in Publication Data

Miller, John William.
    The paradox of cause and other essays.

    CONTENTS: The paradox of cause.—Utopia and the
state.—Accidents will happen. [etc.]
        1. Philosophy—Addresses, essays, lectures.
I. Title.
B29.M1533   1978   191   78–5998
ISBN 0–393–01172–0

                2 3 4 5 6 7 8 9 0

Contents

Note

Of the essays in this volume, two first appeared in *The Journal of Philosophy;* one was a contribution to a symposium at the University of Chicago; two were read, in somewhat different form, before the Harvard Philosophy Club; one was read before the Phi Beta Kappa Society of Hobart College; and one was delivered as a public lecture at Williams College; several of the others were originally composed as letters to friends.

The
Paradox of Cause
and Other Essays

1

The Paradox of Cause

I

The expulsion of mind and purpose from the domain of nature offers no novelty in the history of thought. But in our own day, determinism and mechanism are no longer esoteric beliefs but generally accepted axioms. To be sure, one often encounters pious affirmations of faith in some supernatural agency, in the soul, or in immortality; but such faith has degenerated into a vague hope, into an attractive but hardly defensible aspiration. Nowadays one needs to apologize for teleology, whereas mechanism no longer labors under the burden of proof. Even psychology openly boasts of its emancipation from the ghost-soul and complacently displays its wares in terms of stimulus-response events, where the whole story wins approbation in the measure that it can be restricted to material and mechanical concepts.

Since the seventeenth century this doctrine has acquired force and persuasion. The achievements of science have given it prestige; the order and regularity which it postulates and describes promise to man the chance of power, of control, and of a unified picture of his world. Apparently we cannot rest in meaningless and lawless variety. And, if mechanism thereupon bars us from free participation in the creation of our world and of our fortunes, it seems to offer compensation in the splendid sweep of its intellectual vision.

Mechanism destroys the possibility of freedom. Indeed, where everything is as it must be, nothing can become what it ought to be. Consequently all values in ethics, logic, and esthetics disappear. Weak attempts are often made to save for them, at the very least, the status of pleasant illusions, of useful hypotheses calculated to make living tolerable. One may, of course, wonder how a wholly mechanical world could produce so psychological an event as illusion and error. But apart from that, whoever is smart enough to pierce this veil of subjective deception over the autonomy of values must needs fall back into a pallid stoicism. Consequently there have appeared delicate and emasculated connoisseurs, the apostles of pity, of taste, and of egocentric voluptuousness, who make the universal death more horrible and ghastly by pretending that they are alive.

Very frequently those who persist in the hope of freedom scan heaven and earth for evidences of indeterminism. They feel that the failure of universal causation would give room for freedom. They eagerly greet all scientific difficulties which suggest the breakdown of law and the emergence of an indeterminate spontaneity. Even sober scientists hail the alleged vagrancy of the latest atom with a curious mixture of joy and dread. They rejoice as men that the impregnable wall of necessity has been breached; they dread as scientists the collapse of their intellectual axioms, of their cosmic authority, and of their experimental procedure. Natural vagrancy seems to belittle their office as reporters and spectators of an inevitable process, while reinstating them as creative agents. These are bitter alternatives.

But the failure of causal order offers no hope for freedom. Anarchy in nature excludes power, control, or purpose quite as effectively as does necessity. Indeed, it destroys every shred of security, every opportunity for will. Purpose can neither formulate nor execute itself apart from dependable sequences in nature. Where objects and events possess no regular constitution, no definite sequence, the human will gets no intellectual content in terms of which to assert its direction and its program. How shall one proceed to cure headaches if pain occurs for no reason at all? What drug could the physician recommend? Both head and drug would lose their lawful outlines, would, indeed, cease to be recognizable.

Consequently it is distressing to witness the welcome extended to natural anarchy. By whatever device teleology is to be reinstated it will not be through disorder. And yet, this misdirected hope serves to disclose a lurking discontent over determinism, a discontent usually repressed in polite intellectual discourse, yet ready to show itself timorously upon the slightest suggestion of causal failure.

There is one hope and only one; perhaps we have not understood the character of causal order, perhaps we have a wrong picture of the way in which cause operates and of what makes it possible as a maxim of natural unity.

II

Cause appears to be a principle of order, and hence of unity. It links every event with every other, however indirectly, and every group of events with every other group. Arbitrariness finds no place in nature. There are no island universes and no isolated atoms discontinuous with their neighbors. Each event has its occasion or condition through some other, in accordance with law. No event remains intelligible in itself, a finite absolute, but appeals to what is beyond it for membership in a single comprehensible system. Such is the picture.

But as a matter of fact, no actual event is explained by invoking a causally governed universe. By way of illustration, suppose one substitutes the word "God" for "cause" in order to understand some actual event. It may then be true that what has occurred is God's deed, his purposed decision; but it is also true that no understanding of the given event can be so obtained. For God, by bringing about everything and anything, might, for all we know, create an altogether different world or event. Just why a

given specific fact should occur remains quite unintelligible. Indeed, the well-known outcome of the appeal to
divine management is complete resignation to the inscru-
table. God spoke to Job out of the whirlwind: "Where wast
thou when I laid the foundations of the earth? Declare if
thou hast understanding!" Ours not to reason why, but to
ride blindly and without comprehension into the valley of
death, trusting to a beneficent plan withheld from our pen-
etration. And if we can comprehend no part of the plan
from its actual details, why do we persist in alleging a plan?
It seems intolerably perverse to assert unity where none is
found, and where none can be found due to the finitude of
our point of view and the irrelevance of our human values
to a cosmic scheme. What is designed to provide the maximum intelligibility yields only the maximum ignorance.

The appeal to universal cause is, however, quite as futile
as the appeal to universal purpose, and quite analogous in its
complete defeat of unified order. The specific causal conditions of a given event in nature are not clarified by an assertion of universal causal law any more than by a belief in one
increasing purpose. In either case, what explains everything
explains nothing in particular.

It is the business of science to explain the peculiarities of
events. For this reason, and for this reason alone, it employs the technique of experiment, searching out specific
conditions or causes. Were some conditions not more rele-
vant than others, science would become impossible, for re-
strictions would disappear, impossibility and necessity collapse, and the whole of nature reduce to unconnected and
lawless pluralism.

Consequently, every truly scientific, empirical, and experimental statement applies only to specific events, or to
restricted systems of events. No statement about all events
can be scientific, not because the inductive process cannot
be completed, but because it cannot be begun except in
terms of specific properties of objects. Experimentation
can operate only upon abstracted aspects of specific objects,
never upon the whole world or upon a whole object. We

like to think that science is "concrete" because it deals with the sensory and perceptible properties of objects; but in terms of its logical structure it is abstract because its whole experimental procedure is based upon the exclusion of all properties but the one under examination. Causal order is the systematic unification of such abstract sequences.

Accordingly, cause becomes a principle of unity and of understanding only as it grows from a restricted and finite fact. Except from such a restricted fact, *and from the restricted point of view which it implies,* no causal insight can be won. The word "cause" can have meaning only where we find that meaning exemplified. It is exemplified only in the connection of special facts, and only from a point of view which proceeds from special facts. Causes can be found only in terms of the developing process of discovery; and to imagine this process as complete, to overleap the detailed investigations of special facts in order to picture the world as a *fait accompli,* is to lose all significant causal unity. The point of view which defines causes is relative, restricted, and finite. Causes demand the incomplete. *Causes demand relative disorder.*

Hence the paradox of cause: how can cause be *universal* in its scope, yet *restricted* in its actual incidence? If it is universal in an abstract impersonal way, divorced from the specific, finite, and relative, it explains nothing and reduces to anarchy. If it is not universal, it leaves at least some events outside its scope and again leaves anarchy. If it is restricted to special systems, it loses its cosmic force as unity; if it is not restricted to special systems it makes no sense.

This paradox can be stated in many ways. I will try a few more. Cause pretends to offer us unity and order: but what makes actual causal intelligibility possible is disorder, finitude, restriction; and what makes unity possible is the cancellation of that very disorder, finitude, and restriction. Or again: if cause makes no sense apart from the restricted, what sense does it make when applied to the whole universe of events?

III

The moral of this bit of analysis seems quite obvious: causes occur as an aspect of a dynamic teleological process and nowhere else. They occur in the finding of them; they do not occur in an impersonal and finished world, but only in a world of which the very essence is the adventurous enlargement of a finite point of view. Causal order is one of the basic laws in the development of limited perspectives. For what we know at a given time always bears the marks of the incomplete and forces the exploration of new facts and the formulation of fresh hypotheses. The causal demand controls that process as it concerns natural knowledge. Cause is a dynamic concept because it describes an ideal, the ideal of the intelligibility of nature. For nature is in large part a mystery, and causal coherence is but one of the keys to its progressive solution. If we attempt to make this rule of process a character of a supposedly finished world, we can no longer define the rule.

Consequently we are in a position to reconcile the paradox of cause. Cause must be a principle universally valid, and at the same time applicable only to finite and specific actuality. It must express a character of the whole of nature, but it must view that whole only as the ideal completion of a relative point of view through which actual and specific facts win a detailed and particularized causal ordering. It is a principle regulating the forward sweep of thought from a center to its periphery. Every specific event or object, blind and incomprehensible when isolated, demands a search for those conditions through which it may be controlled and even identified. Indeed, it is through their relations, including causal relations, that finite objects are defined. Consequently, the dynamic property of the causal law is a necessary feature of the very restriction to specific facts without which no actual cause can be denoted. Nothing limited is static. The reason why every event has a cause is found in this intellectual imperfection of everything finite, requiring an ever-developing logic for its integrity and preservation. The way to refute the necessity of universal causation is to demonstrate the possibility of static meanings, i.e., to show a world which is not an order and not governed by law.

And so, it seems that, far from being inconsistent with teleology, cause presumes it. It is defined only in an ideal context. Its locus is the finite world where attention to specific facts demands scrutiny of their connections. And this marching logic defines precisely our own human condition. There is no other world, and certainly no other causally ordered world. In a word, the universality of cause does not imply mechanism; indeed it is just the *necessity of cause which is the ground of the refutation of mechanism.* For the standpoint which alone can define and justify causation is an actual process, organic, spiritual, and teleological. Within that movement causal order is an essential feature. Universal causation is the refutation of mechanism.

Very reputable philosophers have attempted to circumvent the ultimacy of cause by imagining a teleological agency externally directing the course of nature. They call attention to the marvels of the world, they consider why the world is as it is rather than some other way, and they suggest that a purpose or design may be necessary to account for it. This would be a proper effort were it possible to display an impersonal causal order as an accomplished fact upon which to base the inference to purpose. Indeed, it is the assumption of this absolutely objective causal region that underlies the many attempts to reinstate purpose as a more basic agency. But this assumption is false, and the inferences based upon it necessarily futile. To picture a causal world apart from teleology, and then to seek for it a spiritual direction, is to insure defeat if one is logical and magical devices if one is not.

We commonly fail to discriminate between teleology and purpose. The former refers to the ideal tendency through which a world is organized in its fundamental form; the latter denotes the psychological desires which motivate specific deeds. One can explain psychologically why a given scientist seeks out the causes of the weather, and why another deals with the expansion of gases; but there is no psychological explanation for the demand that nature be regular and governed by ideals of order. And because men have observed the irrelevance of cause to psychological purpose they have improperly assumed its irrelevance to an ideal teleological process. This assumption has been a source of great confusion and of many ingenious volumes. It is incorrect to say that the world is governed by impersonal cause; it is also incorrect to say that it is governed by psychological purpose: it is correct to say that it is governed by a law of process, ideal in direction, infinite in potentiality, but always finite in status and in point of view.

It is well to remember that "one cannot stand on a platform outside the universe and snipe at it." There is no such absolute point of view. Yet mechanism, while pluming itself on its cold impersonality, and upon its devotion to scientific methods, is nothing more than a rather crude variety of absolutism. It stands on a platform and snipes at the universe. The mechanist is entitled to his causal postulate, but it is the source of his undoing and not of his justification. To assert cause as a property of an absolutely objective and impersonal region is not a dogmatism; it is nonsense.

In sum, the mechanistic doctrine would kill the world and all that move upon it; we are dead men. Some there are who pretend to be alive, even as they admit that life is an illusion and less than a dream. There is no remedy for the resulting lassitude, inertia, viciousness, and triviality without a revision of premises. One of those premises is the assertion of causal determinism. As a rule the intellectual force of such an axiom seems overpowering, leaving us no recourse save an indefensible faith, or the supposedly fortunate discovery of natural vagrancy. But the paradox of cause sets a problem which offers hope of meeting mechanism on its own ground. For that problem contains a challenge to make good on the idea of intelligible cause viewed as the law of an impersonal objective and finished region. And the above argument urges that it is precisely the intelligence of mechanism which is at fault. There is no such impersonal causal region. All order is process, all process is dynamic, teleological, ideal. That is the order of nature.

2

Utopia and the State

The term *utopia* connotes the impractical. It does not refer to plans that might be carried out but would then prove less satisfactory than some alternative, but rather to a plan that is inherently impossible of accomplishment. It suggests, therefore, distinction between fancy and fact, between what might prove satisfying were the world a different sort of place, and what must be accepted in view of the actual state of affairs. To fly in the face of facts is to be utopian. And it is characteristic of thought to regard the facts as being not at all affected or determined by desire. We can only report them, but we cannot alter them.

To state the meaning of utopia in this way is to condemn it by definition. The world must be conformed to; it cannot be changed. Indeed, faithfulness to the facts seems to call for a renunciation of desires, rather than for a program of action. If we can alter no facts at all there is no further problem. We become wholly determined by the rest of nature, and without any capacity for executing plans or realizing hopes. As a rule, however, the objections to utopia do not go quite that far. They permit such limited schemes as lie within practical attainment. The problem is not generally stated as a conflict between some plans and no plans at all, but rather as between realizable and impossible plans. We are to trim our sails, but we are not necessarily to lie at anchor. Some modest wishes the universe will grant, but no likelihood of complete fulfillment either now or in another world can be entertained. Plato proposed a utopia in his celebrated *Republic;* and while it constitutes for him the perfect state, even its perfection is limited, since it includes the lower classes whose minds or temper unfit them for participation in the full insight of the chosen guardians of public affairs. Outside of theology there are few absolutely perfect societies, and even the Christian heaven has a hierarchy of saints and of angels. So there is a factor of practical limitation even in acknowledged ideal societies. They describe the best that can be done with more or less imperfect material.

In so far as they recognize such restricted success they become less utopian and more realistic. Their motive may have been hard-headed enough, although the result proved mistaken. But in an engineering problem mistakes are always possible, so that the characteristic flavor of the utopian idea does not occur where the failure of a scheme is due rather to a mistaken understanding of possibilities than to a rejection of all limits. It is only where perfection is aimed at and where all the heart's desires have finally come to rest, leaving no residue of yearning, that the true utopian quality is present. For utopia is an assertion of the ideal, and the ideal terminates inadequacy. To do one's best and to acknowledge the poverty, the necessary insufficiency, of that best, is not to be utopian, but to be simply a realistic actor. Half a loaf is better than no bread, and to be content with half seems both the part of modesty and of wisdom. "I dare do all that may become a man," says Macbeth. "Who dares do more is none." There is hazard enough in decidedly restricted programs, and it seems madness to entertain counsels of perfection when no perfection is attainable.

Unfortunately such a view is not the whole truth, although it might be pleasant to think it so. It seems that human nature is not so easily tamed. Indeed, to suppose that one could deal with the contemporary world on that basis would be the very essence of utopian illusion. Men do not set limited goals for themselves. In fact, and in principle, there is no such sort of goal. All particular enterprises occur in the context of something other than their own limits and because of that context. I write these notes because of this lecture, but not for their own sakes. And the lecture is itself no absolute, but fits into a still larger scheme involving college and the place of the college. Any particular act can, in fact, be regarded as purposive and as fulfilling only as it becomes the local vehicle of an essentially boundless program. It is our attempt to meet confusion somewhere, to arrest it for a moment, in order to go on to the next point of challenge. One may counsel limited ambition, but no ambition is absolutely limited, and in the measure that it is strong it can derive its strength only from the desperate urgency of the enterprise into which it fits. Men can move resolutely for particular ends only as larger purposes enforce their local surrogate. Every will attempts the impossible. We are incurably utopian, since we must arm ourselves with boundless resolve in so far as we propose to reach and maintain any goal whatsoever. To cease that activity, to suppose that there is any termination of care and labor is to entertain an illusion and to relapse into a dream. Eternal vigilance is the price of liberty, but also the price of truth. "Does the road wind uphill all the way? Yes, to the very end."

In this way and for these reasons it is not possible to maintain the distinction between the illusion of perfectionist schemes and those of merely limited scope. Neither for us as individuals nor for the social group is that possible. The very truth which we so deeply crave and so highly praise, the truth that is to recommend to us modesty of program and wise restriction of enterprise, is itself dependent upon its perpetual pursuit. There can be truth only where there are no final truths. The preservation of truth requires the functioning of the same resolution that motivates every other desideratum. Truth cannot be separated from will, and to suppose the contrary is to have not truth in its fugitive instability, but dogma. To recommend limited aims, the abandonment of far horizons in the interests of the truth, is to state an inherent contradiction. It is to do more. It is to suppose that one knows the truth, and that one has so thoroughly understood the place of desire in the world that one can portray the absolute. To recommend limited ends when one alleges the possession of final insight is hardly itself a modest attitude. It is, in fact, utopian, since it claims perfection of a sort. On that ground one ought not to condemn it, however, for we are bound to be utopian in one way or another. But we ought rather to consider further whether such a utopia is the true one. The condemnation of utopia can be valid only as the unlimited has been apprehended, and limitation transcended.

It would seem, then, that the idea of utopia is more radical and deep-seated than at first appeared. The initial contrast between the perfectionist ideal where all demands are met and the practical contentment with half a loaf is only superficial. For practice must take on some aspects of utopian perfectionism in order to launch itself effectively. It is not *practical* to engage in limited programs unsupported by some claim that they go beyond the practical. The pragmatism of William James admitted the need of human nature for some "will to believe," for some confidence not only in local enterprise but in the whole of individual life if there was to be hope of determined effort and courageous bearing in the face of difficulties.

Indeed, hazards are not only local. Life itself is a hazard, its prolongation dubious and its effectiveness undemonstrable within its own limits. Its basic hazard is absolute, and to that absolute risk there must be an absolute answer of one sort or another. Such answers have been given. They take two forms: the denial of life, or pessimism; and its affirmation through some sort of utopian ideal.

Pessimism may best be known to the present audience in its psychological form. Freud sees human nature as controlled by two basic forces, as irrational as they are insistent. On the one hand the egoistic appetites lead to assertion of will, and on the other side the libido craves voluptuous nepenthe. But the assertion of will only leads to an unquiet postponement of what it really seeks, namely some masterful poise which is not within the power of effort to attain, no matter how much it may be prolonged. Action, undertaken in the interest of fulfillment, meets more opposition than it can conquer, leading to all manner of attempts to compensate for deficiencies or to repress strong desires. The resultant adjustment takes the form of a retreat from conflict, and consequently seeks a return to that passivity which characterizes pre-natal existence. The Freudian ideal becomes amoeboid, where infinitesimal will meets a minimum of repulse. The celebrated sexual note in Freud describes no vigorously adventurous Don Juan, but rather the decadent passivity of will-less satisfaction. Yet where there is no will at all there is no life at all, and there is no answer save in death. Life seeks the static, not the dynamic, says Freud, and even in its energies, it finds no intrinsic satisfaction. For action means opposition, and opposition is undesired. Thus Freud finds life inherently self-defeating. Desire may be extinguished, but it cannot be fulfilled. Here is an absolute answer to an absolute demand.

Schopenhauer's pessimism grows from the same type of consideration. A student of oriental philosophies, he adopted the doctrine of the futility of the finite will, and sought Nirvana in the unconscious. Weber writes of him, "Since being is synonymous with suffering, positive happiness is an eternal utopia. Only negative well-being, consistency in the cessation of suffering, is possible, and this can be realized only when will, enlightened as to the inanity of life and its pleasures by the intelligence, turns against itself, negates itself, renounces being, life, and enjoyment." Schopenhauer regards the Christian doctrine as also counseling such abdication from will, renunciation of self and desire. This is probably not the case, yet there has been enough of idle dream from sensible practicality. Whatever can be said of Christianity it is not a practical doctrine. It counsels perfection rather than acquiescence.

Pessimism found also a congenial temper in the ancient world, whose three chief ethical systems are all directed at the renunciation of effort. Theognis, the Rousseau of antiquity, the advocate of a back-to-nature movement, sought only to prevent the complication of life and of desire. The Epicureans tried to beat the game by so managing satisfactions as to wring out a maximum of static enjoyment and a minimum of pain. The Stoics, caught in a vast rational providence, could only accept the universe. I am no disciple of Spengler, but I am not above learning something from him, and he has with keen insight detected the essentially static and will-less character of classic civilization. Horace recommended the *aureum mediocritas,* Aristotle's "the golden mean," and all adopted the maxim "nothing to excess." Man was to knock on wood and not try to compete in happiness with the gods, for that would be impious. Socrates, says Hegel, was not the first great student of ethics; he was rather the founder of ethics, for he faced life with a deep unclassical gaiety, and with a belief in the validity of the will seeking ultimate satisfactions in its own right. Plato, of course, is completely out of tune with the temper of his time, and he knew it. He was the first freeman of the western world because he proposed utopia, and a lawful one.

Coming to our own time we might contemplate the figure of Bertrand Russell. He is the author of an essay called "The Free Man's Worship," in a volume entitled *Mysticism and Logic.* In this brilliant, and even magnificent, work he wonders what place human values can have in a world inexorably causal and mechanical in which man is doomed to extinction. There is no place for us, and it is best to crush the longing of our hearts and cease deluding ourselves with cosmic utopias. The cold facts of nature are wholly indifferent to our schemes. But Russell's head, though bloody, is unbowed, and like the dying Beethoven he will shake a defiant fist at the shattering lightning, proclaiming his unconquerable resolve to follow the truth, though the truth may slay him. He will not sell out to delusion. It is too great a pose, too earnest and somber, to be lightly dismissed as melodramatic. For after all he is correct in his assumption that mechanism destroys values. Yet, as F. H. Bradley caustically remarks, "where everything is bad, it must be good to know the worst."

In his *Jardin d'Epicure* Anatole France portrays the doom of all human aspiration, resigning himself to futility and shedding a few restrained tears of pity upon the deluded mass of humanity that so fatuously treats the passing show of action as possessing importance enough to warrant a desperate attack upon the citadels of fulfillment. Professor Carl Becker furnished a further illustration of the plight of values in the context of a rational, or logically ordered world. In his genial book *The Heavenly City of the 18th Century Philosophers* he presents a picture of the rationalistic revulsion from superstition, both in the church and the state. Men were to move God out of the world, and to look upon nature as a closed system on the Newtonian model, where some inexorable law barred the intervention of spiritual powers, and so stripped of authority priest and king who claimed to be the mundane representatives of that power. Then, having banished these fancies, they proposed to ameliorate human life, by making men free and equal, by instituting justice and fraternity. And Becker greatly enjoys the spectacle of these liberators who struggle to reconcile a naturalistic determinism with an ethical doctrine of progress. In his celebrated novel *The Magic Mountain,* Thomas Mann presents the vivid figure of Settembrini, rationalist and humanist, caught in this same dilemma. For the rigorous order of nature reduces to subjective prejudice the special recipe for the social utopia to which Settembrini devotes his life.

In sum, the escape from dream and illusion, the realistic drive toward practicable ends, toward limited control and power, has, on the stage of history, tended rather to instate a new dream, a new utopia, in the place of what offered itself initially with so much confidence as the healthy region of practical action. And it is worth making a somewhat systematic point, namely that there is no problem of utopia in so far as discussion is confined to the practical against the impractical. It is only when the status of the practical is itself called into question and a justification sought for its claim to healthy-minded fulfillment that the issue becomes important, and a solution could be proposed. On the level of limited success or failure no one wants to fail, and there is no debate. It is only as the principle of the limited success is examined that one becomes aware of the utopian background of such limited practicality. If to be utopian is to be blind, to blink the facts, to rush for satisfaction regardless of what the truth may be, then the practical life may become only another indulgence, another dogmatic and subjective assertion of values, accidentally disguised by superficial movement, but to the discerning eye inherently bankrupt and no better than any other dream.

And it seems fair to say that men of action often do appear as the very personification of utopians, in so far as their schemes appear to us as dogmatic and subjective. They are making their dreams come true, but nevertheless *their* dreams are not ours, and consequently cannot win approbation from what we prefer to regard as the truth and the real. This is an everyday consideration wherever men meet to discuss plans, or conflict in their execution. "A hair, perhaps, divides the false and true," and actuality from the illusion.

These examples may serve to bring out the picture of the pessimistic renunciation of life either in the interests of avoiding its fruitless turmoil or because the world is so made as to bar the belief in values. And perhaps it is now possible to claim that the real debate is over value or no value, rather than between utopian values and practical values. Value is a utopian ideal. It is absolute or it is nothing; for if it is not absolute the intellect can always find ways of reducing it to a futile illusion or to a realization in nothing short of death.

I said above that an absolute risk must get an absolute answer, and I have paraded some examples of the pessimistic type of reply to life's demand for fulfillment. But there are positive replies, and they are utopian.

All positive answers to this question go beyond the intellect. It becomes obvious at once that values or hopes are not really that until they are affirmed, and that their affirmation is not a matter of logic but of action. Somewhere in all positive utopias action is involved, and only in the fiat of the deed can the value of the deed be established. Action can never be proved sensible. It can only be the *actuality* of sense. Perhaps it can be put another way: to contemplate action from the passive point of view of logic where nothing happens is simply to miss the place where values occur, and where they become real, namely in the deed. But in the deed they assert a finality which no amount of reasoning can either bestow or remove. The intellectual fallacy derives from the very attempt to ask the question about the reality of value. There is no possible way of deciding that question by looking about one in the world. For after all the decision rests with the inquirer, and since, by hypothesis, he has never encountered any actual value, he cannot very well know what he is looking for. But if he should claim that he knows what value is, but not whether there is any in fact, one might ask him why he is inquiring. For the inquiry could occupy him only in so far as it was worth his while. His inquiry is itself an assertion of value, and there is no finding it elsewhere. Without our taking a stand, values could not occur to us, but if we do stand, then we have asserted the actuality of value.

Perhaps an illustration will best show this point. In Joseph Wood Krutch's book *The Modern Temper* he offered one of the pessimistic stories previously described. He says, for example, that there can be no tragedy in the modern world because our world-picture, being mechanistic and deterministic, can no more allow for defeat than for success. Defeat means the failure of an ideal, and there are no ideals. He has a chapter called "Love, or the Death of Value" where he shows the futility and meaninglessness of such a feeling in a world indifferent to aspirations. He proposes either successful life as uncouth brutality, or else a decadent and doomed sophistication, and adduces historical evidence to support this thesis. It was a fine argument, workmanlike, informed, subtle, urbane, and cogent. Later, however, he appeared in another volume called *Was Europe a Success?*, and he asked that question in the interest of bringing out the peculiar merits of European culture. He found those merits in the rich European flowering of individuality, in freedom of speech, of property, of emotion, and in the resultant aesthetic products. But it is that peculiar achievement of European culture which he sees menaced by the dogmatic encroachments of communism and fascism, and against the destruction of all that he treasures he rebels. He could not do otherwise and be himself, for he is a liberal, a skeptic, and something of an artist. Totalitarian states bring him to bay, and he so far forgets his stoical indifference, or his Epicurean skepticism, as to come very close to a cry. Mr. Krutch now affirms, and no skeptic should do that. All his fine arguments go into the discard in a wholly non-logical assertion of values. But what else can he do? Of course it is nonsense to object to the institutions based on a materialistic interpretation of history where a mechanical or disorderly world makes *all* history meaningless since there is no will or destiny freely unfolding itself in events. But this episode exemplifies the difficulty of maintaining a wholly neutral attitude and of finding values apart from their affirmation. And while decision and action always express some measure of desperation, and so never win to perfection of controlled elegance, they also express the condition of our own existence. Indeed, there seems little use arguing the point that a free man, who, to be free, must be an end and not a means, can only find value in his own autonomy, and hence in his fiat to pursue values. For what is an end in itself can be that only as it freely asserts its unconditioned validity.

On the whole, education stresses the intellect. It deals with assertions for which one must apologize. But for that reason it produces in many men a paralysis of will. The orthodoxy of the time scouts the possibility of any finalities, and hence sterilizes the will and destroys its ardor. There are, of course, reasons for this. We tend to find in the past so much error, ignorance, and greedy lust for power that we have become more alert to the likelihood of error than confident of the possibility of any truth. And so the intellect casts its withering glance upon all these rash pretenders to truth and value. We emphasize criticism rather than creation, and tend to frown on any free originality, to patronize it, and to treat it as another well-meant but rather troublesome folly. Our public men are all very clever, but few speak words that are arresting in their clear disclosure of some commitment for which their author will stand, and if necessary go down to defeat. We have ceased to believe in it. Even the revolutionaries don't quite mean it; they have to refresh their resolution by means of some-body's theories, and it is not necessary to fear the tenta-tiveness of such attitudes. They can always be overborne.

In describing the character of Theodore Roosevelt, Henry Adams writes as follows in his *Education:* "Power, when wielded by abnormal energy, is the most serious of facts. Roosevelt, more than any other living man within the range of notoriety, showed the singular primitive qual-ity that mediaeval theologians assigned to God—he was pure act." Yes, such power *is* the most serious of facts because, confronting it, we must take our own resolve and stand for ourselves. It is not that we must stand for this or that, but rather that we must stand for something, make *some* answer whether to agree or to differ, and we must make it freely or else it is not our answer and so not a sign of any personality. If one wants to be a person one must as-sume the burden of such affirmation. Most of us never quite mean it. And even what looks like emphasis and force from the outside may be in fact a personal technique rather than the heart of quiet resolution. But in so far as one en-counters persons capable of such unfaltering assertion one has met a genius, and life flows the more strongly in us for it. There are, of course, very few such persons. But they are the ones who live and who justify life, and so they call the rest of us back to new courage. This was a quality of Lincoln's, and I like E. A. Robinson's lines very much:

> Was ever master yet so mild as he
> And so untamable?

So mild, and so untamable; a mildness that is possible only *because* the resolution is beyond question, and so calls for no assurances of its power. But untamable persons are dan-gerous, disturbing. The old bottles cannot hold their new wine. And we so dull the edge of resolution by insisting upon a moribund and leering intellectualism. It is safe, but it is decadent. Sometimes we try to compensate for all that by organizing a cheering section of one sort or another, but I find that a person is more likely to drink a cup of coffee with conviction than to give the lone cheer with hearty committal.

This seems a long way from Mr. Krutch. But you may recall that having stated the issue between value and no values at all, and having illustrated the negative type of answer from the numerous pessimists, we turned to the way in which positive affirmation might be possible, using the career of Mr. Krutch as an example of a man brought to bay, and showing that only in that primitive, absolute, and terrible assertion of will could values be found. If this picture seems a bit rough for the academic scene, it may only go to prove that the academic is utopian. Certainly nothing is more utopian than to pretend that human nature can be understood or met otherwise than in this context of assertion. It is just that free assertion that *is* human nature, and while logic is indispensable, and engineering useful, they do not exhaust the personality. For that matter, the pursuit of truth is itself a gesture of will, and usually a very romantic affirmation, rather than a consciously abstract factor in the whole man. Truth is an enterprise, perpetually unfinished, tentative, hypothetical; and it seems blind to the point of perversity that those who try to tell the truth so often overlook the fact that they are *telling* it, and that they can denote no single proposition called true apart from the absolute affirmation of a will that proposes to discipline its ardor to this endless ideal. It is good philosophic technique to pay out plenty of rope until the very heat of denial stares into the face of him that makes it and causes a realization of both his bid for freedom and of its responsibility. *Truths* do not make us free, but the truth is our freedom, for it occurs only in the context of a declaration that has no justification but its own life. We do not die for truths, we argue about them; but for the chance of telling any truths at all we stage revolution and proclaim utopia. Utopia is inevitable; it inheres in the actuality of any person.

The forces that we must meet are not only in individuals but in social groups, in nations, races, churches, or political parties. In so far as we need pay attention to such groups we must see their thought or theory backed by the will to realize or make actual its programs. It may come to blows; for a strong insurgency is only the sign of a strong life and as we value ourselves we cannot fail that rendezvous at some disputed barricade. For it is the nature of the will to strike, and it has no reality from that implicit readiness to take whatever medicine may be necessary. The will cannot sell out and still remain. And the real place of systematic pessimism in thought is its profound and horrid obscenity. It is death masquerading as life.

It was Hegel's idea that a turning point was reached in the history of cultures when death was seen as the sole condition for an absolute affirmation of life, and the sole evidence of a belief in life. And those are the great ones who have not hesitated to affirm their ideals in that way. By an instinct that outtops logic all men stand arrested by that spectacle, and pause for a silent moment as they savor the quiet that broods over outer tumult.

Before leaving this endlessly varied theme of the absolute will, it might be useful to point out that basically we do not judge men by moral codes, and that we spontaneously suspect a person who too often refers his deeds for rational approbation. Upon Shakespeare, Beethoven, Goethe, Michaelangelo; upon Pericles, Augustus, or Lincoln; upon Plato, Newton, or Ben Franklin, a moral judgment is an irrelevant impertinence. Others abide our question; they are free. And they are that because they reached out for rich experience with eager hands and were above a niggardly moral economy and the miserly weighing out of personal satisfactions. In his distorted way, Nietzsche saw this point and developed his superman. But that monster lived by a theory, and had to keep reminding himself, not that he was alive, but that God was dead. And so he is a sapless, humorless, and joyless creature. Zarathustra's ten years of meditation on the mountain bore only this sour fruit. The superman is a dead man, because he lives by the intellect. We need not worry about him. He can be tamed, because he can be argued with. He is not a genius.

The turn from negation to affirmation is unquestionably very terrible to consider. The forces it lets loose seem mad, arbitrary, and uncontrollable. In any case, they are disturbing, and it is only natural to try to put them down. We are likely to become drunk with sight of power and loose wild tongues that deny the law. But one thing is certain: that assertion must occur, and so it is equally certain that it can be met only by a counterthrust equally strong and even more persistent. An absolute assertion can get only an absolute answer if it is to be controlled. The concrete actuality that gives that answer is the state. For the state is the objectification of the conditions of the will to power. In sum, and in conclusion, it seems possible now to stress the point that the utopian character of the will is not due to some intellectually constructed heavenly city at which that will aims. What is more, no such heavenly city would enlist the deeds of the will except as it recommended itself to values already accepted. The will is utopian only because it asserts its own freedom. Consequently one is now in a position to point out the reason why all intellectual utopias fail to be quite convincing. They fail because, as intellectual constructs, they could at best merely interpret a demand laid down in advance, but being interpretations of an absolute hunger for experience and power they must necessarily prove unsatisfactory. For no infinite appetite can be quenched by particular goods. All that particular utopias can do is to *destroy* the very will to which they owe their own creation. Men are incurably utopian because no specific utopia can bring unquestioning sufficiency. Says Troilus to Cressida,

This is the monstrosity in love, dear lady,
That the will is infinite, and the execution confined,
That the desire is boundless, and the act a slave to limit.

The utopian heart of man is thus identical with his necessarily asserted freedom. But it takes a long time and much actual suffering for mankind or any individual to discover that fact. And I do not have any great hope of making the idea persuasive except in so far as any one who may be listening can find that this is the truth about himself. If one stands off and tries to prove it, it is gone, because it has then become the unconscious and unrecognized urge that directs the proof, but does not fall within the proof. Before intellectual utopias we need not feel reverence; but before this authentic finality of freely asserted personality everyone must make his obeisance. Few have it in sufficient degree to arrest our attention, but where we do see life flowing strongly, courageously, and with an intensity that goes beyond pleasure and beyond good and evil, we must pause in wonder. History is the unfolding of this search for freedom as manifested in institutions and in art. That, however, is another theme, too large for present purposes.

Before going on to a further development of this idea of the state, it might be well to review some of the intellectual utopias with which most persons are familiar. They fall into two groups, utopias of the past, and utopias of the future. To be sure, Leibnitz and others have proposed that the present is also perfect in the best of all possible worlds, but while Voltaire's criticism of this idea in *Candide* is thoroughly superficial it seems fair to say that the present, being the locus of unfulfilled desire, lies outside the sort of utopian scheme in question.

As utopias of the past, may be instanced Heaven before creation, or at least before the revolt of the angels, the Garden of Eden, and the golden age of man portrayed in Plato's dialogue *The Statesman*. For the future there stands Heaven, Nirvana, such societies as are found in Plato's *Republic,* the *Utopia* of Sir Thomas More, Edward Bellamy's *Looking Backward,* perhaps the communistic society, and many others.

With regard to utopias of the past there is a striking common property, namely that they represent the state of affairs prior to some fall from grace. In the Christian story of Heaven and of the Garden of Eden, there is no point and no story until the devil appears, whether as the ambitious Lucifer, or as the subtle serpent. Without the fall there could have been no sin, no redemption, no death, judgment, or final reward. The persistence of this idea in religion and philosophy, its association with distinguished minds rather than with weak charlatans, and the tendency toward its natural and effortless acceptance by millions of men may well bring one to treat it as something more than a pretty invention or gratuitous conjecture.

For example, Plato, as everyone knows, found in temporal life no adequate explanation of his so-called "ideas" or universals, and consequently saw no merely natural foundation for logical or ethical principles; yet he observed that as a matter of fact even an uneducated slave boy could somehow out of his own resources solve problems in geometry, being already possessed of innate logical principles. Consequently he regarded earthly life as a fall from a condition of pure spirituality, as a degradation of a purer state of disembodied soul. Again, Plotinus regarded the natural universe with its change, variety, and imperfection as an emanation of a perfect divinity, and like Plato saw the human tasks as an attempted return to God. Even Aristotle placed God prior to nature, viewing the latter as not quite equal to the divine in perfection. Of course the Christian story follows the same pattern.

In all these views, the perfection derives from perfection. The fall is due to sin, and in any case brings sin in its wake. Sin seems to destroy perfection, and only for that reason is evil. Were there no assumed perfection there could be no corruption, no error, and no conscience. In the parable of the prodigal son the return is marked by confession: "Father, I have sinned against Heaven and before thee," and the poignancy of that surrender turns upon the sense of loss. Thus, it is necessary to begin with the ideal in order to discover the failure to realize it in detail. A condition of projecting a future utopia is not only present inadequacy, but the golden age of innocence. In the context of merely finite ends there is only failure, not failure in principle. But just as error is no practical shortcoming, neither is sin. Both stand for the collapse of integrity. A logical error is troublesome, confusing, and clouding only as it infects the whole of one's knowledge and the clarity of a world of experience. Error destroys not a thought, but thought. As the books say, "If George Washington crossed the Rubicon, then the moon is made of green cheese," i.e., the radical incoherence of the antecedent with all that we know of history is so destructive of good sense that all rules are off and anything at all is tolerated. Whirl becomes king. In the same way, sin, deficiency, desires, point to no local and finite imperfection, but rather to some clouding of a postulated and essential wholeness. Criticism, without which neither logical nor volitional shortcomings could be alleged, requires final and absolute standards. And because self-consciousness cannot be achieved at one step, the ideal by which the actual is measured was put into a region of time or of existence, prior to the actual. Plato's struggle with this difficulty is one of the masterly pilgrimages of inspired thought. For although he ended by endowing the real with finality, he had begun, as we all know, by placing all ideas and ideals in a heavenly place out of changing and the temporal. Indeed, the alienation of the ideal to the actual was necessary in order that the problem of their conciliation could occur or be solved, and utopias of the past are the mythological form of a necessary problem and of its equally necessary answer.

There is a further property of these past utopias which should be brought out. Without limitation or deficiency there is no time, no change, no process, no history. It seems that this has been implicitly recognized in all these stories. Past utopias are static; so too are all utopias of the future, although this latter fact has not been systematically recognized. Because Adam and Eve desired to know good and evil they were cast out of Eden. They craved to become like God, and one cannot blame them for that. The serpent deserves a vote of thanks and not the opprobrium heaped upon him. For only as man was tempted and fell, could he realize the meaning of his values and begin the desperate struggle to recapture them. In the Persian religion of Zoroaster, there is staged a great contest between light and darkness. In Plotinus the created world alone has variety, movement, direction. Anything we could identify as thought or desire presumes this scene of the unfinished enterprise, this curious antithesis of finite and infinite. And perhaps I may add that the Christian faith has made the incarnation of the divine, its limitation to human form, a central tenet. Perfection is only the imperfect aware of its status. Thus the necessities of actual endeavor require the utopian concept of perfection as well as its dissipation into the actual, i.e., into the world of change and appearance. And instinctively we reject utopias of the future just because they cancel and annul one of the necessary conditions of satisfaction, namely, the desperate assertion of a limited and unfinished will. For in that assertion value is literally created, and hence wins its freedom.

Finally, in this situation we may note that a future utopia thus derives from the assumption of a past one. There is no longing for a golden tomorrow where the perfect has not already existed, and hence now exists, since it cannot be destroyed. A gloomy present without the postulated past utopia can see no glowing promise. "And tomorrow, and tomorrow, and tomorrow, there's this little street, and this little house," wails Edna Millay amidst the ashes of life. Matthew Arnold in a world that lies about him with such apparent enticement, can see it only as "a darkling plain, . . . where ignorant armies clash by night."

In sum, utopias proposed as past bear witness to the presence of the idea in the actual, to the necessity of the fall, and to the dependence of history, human or divine, upon limitation. They show the craving of men for both a limited personality, knowing good and evil, and the cancellation of that limit in the future. But because that cancellation would only recreate the story of Adam and Eve, it can win only qualified approval. Thus, the present, and that alone, is both the locus of any valid utopia, and of its negation in unfulfilled desires. But great men overcome that limit by recognizing it, and so generate nobility out of their bondage. To do that is to be free. The great do not apologize; they are affirmers of finalities.

What has so far emerged is a picture of human nature incurably utopian, not because it is vagrant or irresponsible, not because it prefers dreams to reality, but rather because the hard actuality of any specific deed contains in itself, as a condition of its own persisting force, some assumption of an ideal. Utopias of the past and future are merely the symbols of this necessity. There are no remote finalities, but there are present ones, hidden in the living reality of any actual deed, and compelling just in the measure that the deed drives onward with persistent power. For the bankruptcy of finite deeds can get clear only as they are first desperately undertaken and the illusion of final and static satisfaction thereby disclosed. As a result, one is thrown back upon some intrinsic validity of the will itself, not for a certification of its value by some result external and accidental to it. We can only assert value, we cannot *attain* it or *prove* it as an incident to our own selfhood, or to our running experience in this world or another. And it would seem that this self-containment with the fierce fearlessness that it implies is the distinguishing mark of all gallant minds. And when a person has died, and it comes time to pronounce a eulogy, it is just this quality upon which we fasten. Particular attainments or failures fall away into insignificance before the spirit that empowered them. This, of course, is wholly impractical and utopian, but it is nevertheless the only consideration that sustains the practical. Utopia is the symbol of *responsibility,* not of vagrancy, and it seems fair to say that where there is no utopian belief there is no trusting anybody. That is the true vagrancy, the true irresponsibility, the true subjectivism of dogmatic dreams.

What is called for, obviously, and what I here only sketchily supply, is an application of this utopian orientation of desire to the state. For in so far as utopia is regarded as having any earthly significance it must involve satisfactory conditions within actual experience. Perhaps I have shown too much concern with the general idea of utopian felicity, and not enough with present proposals. Yet, such a background is not without its good side, since it puts up a few warning signs and offers some counsel about impossible plans.

Theories of the state can be classified into those that describe a status, and those that define a process. As an example of the first, consider Plato's *Republic*. Plato was much concerned over the individualism, skepticism, and anarchy of his time and in the first two books of the *Republic* gives as fine a picture as we have of the radical and lawless individualism where might makes right. But he felt that the will did not get what it wanted in such impulsive deeds, and that to be really free it must find a principle of mastery and of restraint beyond the natural man. The true desire of man is justice, he held, because only in justice can one avoid that disorder that frustrates the will and prevents its fulfillment. But Plato's *Republic* describes an essentially static society. It contains neither the rules for bringing it about, nor for modifying it once it has been established. It is out of time, and ahistorical. It does not describe the scene in which men come to themselves, by the trial-and-error process of knowing both good and evil, as a condition of appreciating the good. This static society eliminates anarchy, private assertion, and freedom, since it removes private property and liberty of expression. Plato, as everyone knows, banishes the artists, just as modern communists or fascists allow only the officially approved art. He leaves no room for the anarchy, disorder, and injustice. And just as he furnishes no method for instituting utopia, he likewise furnishes none for going beyond it. This too is a mark of all authoritarian states; they can be inaugurated only by arbitrary force, and by the same force overthrown. They do not define the conditions on which the will to power can assert itself, and for that reason they can offer no freedom. In a sense, all static utopias are a sign of decadence, and of abdication. They do not describe the scene of patient progress where minds must be met and convinced. They allow for no tolerance because they have no instruments for converting conflict into agreement. They offer only an absolute choice between complete acquiescence or none, and really between acquiescence and death, or at best exile. For Plato exiled the artists, just as Stalin sent dissenters into Siberia, and Hitler took them into protective arrest or else performed a blood-purge. Finished utopias can do nothing else. They must deny the will, except the subjective will of the autocrat.

Disciples of communism do not like autocrats if you ask them, but that is only because in a communistic state all communists are insiders and so do not anticipate the oppressive hand. But nevertheless they are not free men. They have no rights, neither have they duties. The sign of a right is safe dissent and opportunity for winning one's way with ideas. The sign of duty is safe opportunity for offering one's individual best, even though it be at first unacceptable. There is a great illusion prevalent on this point, namely that duty can be defined as absolute submission to a previously defined mass will. On the contrary, duty has no force save as the individual accepts it freely, and executes it in his own way. There may even be a duty to dissent, a duty to rebel, to differ, to propose new schemes; but in no static utopia can such freedom be acknowledged. It must cancel the very freedom in the interests of which it was proposed.

What advocates of the totalitarian state are afraid of is the absolute anarchy of the individual will. Consequently communists talk about the class struggle. Those who possess are so constituted that no force of argument or education can bring a relinquishment of their possessive greed, and hence they must be violently dispossessed. If this is not what they mean, then I cannot understand their complaints about the oppression exercised, for example, by the newspaper capitalists. If the latter can be brought round by the usual methods, nothing is fundamentally unsatisfactory, and a great victory lies ahead of us as we patiently and intelligently whittle away special privilege. But I venture to point out that the despair of free government is found in just those persons who do not regard the state as a procedure calling for patience and sacrifice, but rather as an inherently arbitrary institution for the protection of one group or another. The class struggle, on that basis, is only the substitution of one arbitrary advantage for another. There certainly is no color of justice in simply overriding those who define their advantage in their own way. And the fact that the masses are many and the capitalists few gives absolutely no moral quality to a preference for the former. It is an arbitrary and subjective choice. But the

anarchy of the individual will is not abolished by transferring power. One can extinguish the individual will, but
then why talk of freedom, morality, justice, rights, and the
rest? For such concepts mean nothing at all save as affirmed
by persons who are free.

In a communistic or any authoritarian state, there can be
no injustice. This may seem to be a high recommendation,
but it is a condition purchased at the cost of justice as well.
All acts are validated by an abstract good will, and by that
alone. There is only one crime, opposition to the arbitrary.
To abolish injustice is to carry justice down with it. This is
not to say that anyone wants a specific injustice to persist,
but it is to say that the conditions which define justice must
permit injustice as well. If one objects to a specific injustice
the way is open in a free state to effect a remedy. That way
will not be obvious or easy, but only as the way is taken can
even the assertion of injustice be demonstrated. Just so, a
judicial process actually defines justice because it is a *process,*
and there is no way of determining that an injustice has occurred without the labor of trial, any more than an assertion
can be called true which has not won its way in the context
of controversy and test.

The second type of political order is the liberal state.
There is no use in pretending that such a state is always possible, or that it can ever be fully attained. But that is the
reason why it is both realistic and ideal or utopian. It may
well be that trouble, disorder, poverty, or ignorance may
so beset a society that for the moment there can be no way
back to order except through autocracy. But it seems fair to
say that while one may admit that order is better than disorder, the state of affairs that requires autocracy is deplorable
and the mark of moral immaturity. Nobody knows
whether in this country we are really safely launched on the
utopian ideal of liberalism. If rich men alone were stupid
and greedy the answer would be clear; but poor men seem
often not a bit better in their own motives, and just as eager
to seize power for their own gain, or to vote for those who
offer garages and chickens. There are many well-inten-
tioned persons who confuse politics with social welfare,

and they are troublesome just because they are generous and high minded.

The liberal state can do no more than offer an arena for the solution of difficulties and of injustice. It is a school of the will, permitting both private property and free speech, but perpetually seeking to reconcile particular conflicts and local injustice. It allows for relative anarchy and for waste. But it is the only answer to the bid for power which men must make, and the only condition under which they could assert a social or moral will. That the will is social can be discovered only by trial, and everyone must make that trial for himself. There is no vicarious morality.

In sum, utopia suggests itself originally as a conflict be-tween practicality and dream. But the practical will reduces to pessimism, or else must arm itself for action by some picture of the ideal. Those ideal conditions will appear as ei-ther past or future and must so appear before the problem can be fully faced. But in the living moment of assertion resides the true absolute. It describes no *fait accompli,* but an endeavor, and a procedure. When that will knows itself it becomes social, for its freedom can escape subjectivity only as it recognizes its limitation in the will of others. The ob-jectification of that freedom is the liberal state, where by patience and labor the free will gives open testimony of its disinterestedness and impartiality. There it finds both its rights and its duties. That seems to be the direction of the utopian urge which no one who is free can escape.

3

Accidents Will Happen

For idealism the problem of the datum offers peculiar difficulty. The datum represents the accidental content of experience, the events which cannot be inferred from abstract order. Data stand for the empirical, the unpredictable, the surprising, the novel, the upsetting, the catastrophic.

Thus data seem an effect produced upon the mind by something alien to itself. They show the mind as passive or receptive, not its own master, not self-contained or self-generating. Nature in all its phases becomes a construction imposed on data. Idealism has been relatively strong in so far as it claims for the mind the laws in accordance with which data are ordered; it has been weak in not exploiting the accidental, or non-rational, as a necessary aspect of that order. For a mind does its work by thinking, by arranging, organizing, and testing, by subduing disorder to thought, will, and feeling. Consequently, no idealism, just in so far as it offers a dynamic conception of the mind, can avoid the fact of accidental data. The pressure of this problem is evident in the type of solution which leading idealists like Royce and Bradley have proposed. At the last they present an absolute who is a "problem solver" with all the answers known, a mind no longer open to surprises, no longer confronted by its "other," no longer beset by that restless incompletion without which it fades into an inarticulate totality, without focus, and so without limitation. To the absolute mind all is immediately given, and even time is metamorphosed into a "totum simul" where it ceases to have any of those features of form without which idealism is bankrupt. Thus, idealism, based on the priority and absoluteness of form, loses its appeal as soon as that form no longer applies to the accidental. Yet, to preserve the accidental is also to preserve what seems alien to mind, some not-mind, from which is derived the varied content which form articulates. And that alien factor, that datum which gives form its task and its force, seems accidental to the self which apprehends it.

I

Characteristic of the discovery of data is the situation of the scientist looking through the microscope and discovering an object not visible to the naked eye; or the watcher of the skies when a new planet swims into his ken. In terms of his already established world there is no reason to anticipate what in detail he discovers. Some discoveries may, of course, be expected on the basis of data already possessed, although the partiality and inherent limitation of any given data forbid flawless or absolute prediction about the next moment; for while the observed event seems required by the hypothesis, so also does the event observed lend assurance to the premises. Indeed, the hypothetical status of premises is sufficient warrant for acknowledging an accidental element in the actual appearance of the conclusion.

But in this picture there is assumed an observer already equipped with content. His mind is not a blank. The accidental datum wins its status as accident, discloses its unpredictable aspect, in terms of the content already possessed. The appearance of accidents to a point of view already furnished with content not only fails to separate the mind from its content, but requires a mind already supplied with it as a condition of describing the accidental status of any actual novelty. But if one is to assume content in order to define the accidental there is no warrant for treating content as in principle accidental. One does not lay bare the force of the problem of accidental data if at the outset one assumes a situation for which data are required. The force of the problem is disclosed only as all data, all content, all particulars are made in principle irrelevant to the point of view which apprehends them. Content could be in principle accidental to the perceiver only as he could be defined in its complete absence. It is not enough to point out that any particular content is an accident; one needs to show that the sort of thing that content is, the sort of factor that it contributes to knowledge, is an accident to the perceiver.

But a subject without content can exhibit none of the psychological functions. It does not remember, feel, or act. Neither observation nor introspection can disclose it. Without content it cannot exist because it cannot function; and its form disappears with the repudiated content. The subject is discovered only as content is differentiated into the private and the public. In the history of philosophy the individual self emerges in the context of doubt over the impersonality of some content, where the privacy of some content is thrown into relief. Skepticism appears with the illicit indictment of all content as private. Thus, accidental content becomes a condition for the discovery of the subject.

Just as there is no passive subject absolutely distinct from content, so neither is there any definable region from which data can be given to such a subject.

The search for an objective region of data is extremely plausible. Yet the objective has always offered difficulties in the history of philosophy. It hardly seems the same as the actual picture of nature now entertained, nature with just these specific objects, and with just these laws of change. For when we make this objective region specific we encounter the possibility of error. Nature, to be sure, stands for the objective and impersonal; but this is not to be identified with the total removal from subjectivity of any given account of what nature specifically is.

Indeed, the nature we now have, far from being the source of data, is rather their interpretation, the result of organizing and testing them. But in advance of this reception and organization there is no region of nature already known from which the accidental data emerge and to which they must be traced. Nature is not first known, and then observed in its piecemeal disclosure of itself to a subject. There is no omniscient point of view to which the occurrence of data ceases to be accidental as their course from source to percipient is traced. Indeed, the occurrence of data requires that they shall have no knowable source; for were that source understood there would be no further accidents, and what are now called accidents would revert to the necessities of a world seen as a *fait accompli,* and so data could no longer be perceived as accidents.

There is no analogy between particular explanations and the explanation of all particulars. In the former case no final release from the accidental is secured. The assumptions which explain are themselves particular and accidental; the event to be explained is one item in the field of organized data; the force of the explanation, rather than abolishing the accidental status of the datum to be explained, requires that it shall retain that status of accidental discovery as a condition of the validity of the explanation. It seems obvious that the explanation of particular accidents draws its force from the preservation of the accidental in principle, and would lose all force if the accidental were explained away in principle. On the assumption that accidents will happen, one may explain how it comes about that the accidental factor of experience secures just this particular embodiment; but if one gets rid of the accidental, neither is there anything to explain, nor any force in the ground of the explanation. Both are accidental, and the power of the explanation is precisely in their common linkage as accidents. Order is the linkage of accidents; and where there are no accidents there is no order.

The source of data is invoked in order to provide a ground for appearance, a ground not itself subject to the charges that can be brought against appearances. And the ground of all appearance can never, accordingly, be either an actual or a possible appearance. Kant was entirely correct in declaring the thing-in-itself unknowable. Appearances can be explained only by appearances.

In sum, it is possible to define neither a blankly passive psychic recipient for data, nor an equally blank absolute object from which data proceed. And there seems, too, a systematic ground for giving up the attempt to be logical or "scientific" or "empirical" about appearance; for in the nature of the case it cannot be traced back to an alien intelligible source. The authority of explanation requires that there be accidents; and consequently it is meaningless to attempt an explanation of the accidental in principle.

II

It is often urged that the accidental is a surprise to the point of view that apprehends it, and the fact of surprise is used to infer the independence of the data from the subject.

Thus surprise also becomes absolute. But there is no absolute surprise. Surprise requires the upsetting of anticipation, and thus assumes both form and content. It is the mark of an experience for which data are presumed. It does not challenge them in principle, nor demand an explanation of them in principle.

There are, furthermore, many surprises that do not go beyond the self. Unexpected proclivities, defects, and aptitudes lurk in us all, and the more upsetting and exhilarating surprises of life are reserved for these arresting revelations of one's own character. Any assertion of the will, any reaching out for the forbidden fruit of the tree of knowledge, drives one out of Eden and condemns not only to the sweating brow but to the troubled heart.

In its more systematic aspects personality also discloses novelties. That liberty involves limitation, that thought does not slay feeling, that logical proof defeats certainty, that self-assertion is social, that self entails the not-self . . . all these ideas, whether true or false, may stir puzzlement, incredulity, or opposition. The self is a surprise to itself.

And one finds in the beauty of art, or in the grace and courage of persons, the most amazing revelations unsuspected, unimaginable, challenging, and humbling. In comparison, the surprises of nature seem trivial, dull, unmoving. Or shall we say that we have learned nothing about the self, that no novelties and no miracles of creation have occurred, and that all discovery is confined to the not-self? Yet even the discovery of the self by skepticism refutes such a position. In short, surprise is not an idea that can be used to define the locus of the not-self. Quite as much it lurks in thought and feelings, and nowhere more dramatically than in creative activity and personal quality.

As for the not-self (nature, for example), completely surprising data destroy it in principle. Indeed it is rather extraordinary that after all these years David Hume should be so disregarded. The reduction of experience to a stream of alleged consciousness, where the complete atomicity of data obliterates all meaning from transcendental origins, leaves no ground for defining even a question about their origin. The passive subject can find neither subject nor object. And data become neither subjective nor objective, but just absolutely and atomically themselves. To make data surprising to an assumed subject is a pretty fallacy indeed; for it assumes as a condition of data a subject which would not find itself in such materials, the only materials at its disposal. The argument from surprise must, of course, allege a transcendental object, because it can be stated only by assuming a transcendental subject. It is no surprise that realists find data surprising. It is remarkable that there should be talk about a subject when, by hypothesis, all content is accidental, unpredictable, unsystematic, and lawless. The whole idea of treating data as in principle accidental to a subject is a flat incoherence. For in such terms there are neither data nor subject, nor any ground for their distinction.

Complete passivity of a subject levying no demands, sunk in flaccid inertia, asking no questions, and formlessly hospitable to anything and everything, renders it incapable of surprise. Until a subject acts it cannot even define objects, for an assertion or definition denotes the consequences of an act, a sequence of experiences attendant upon volition, and hence upon assumed order. It is a pseudo-empiricism that takes its stand in the passive subject, and no empirical declaration is possible in passivity. For empiricism is test, and test is act, and act assumes the law which defines its possibility, spatial law, temporal law, causal law, a world where not anything can happen and not all rules are off. The association of empiricism with passivity can only destroy empiricism as a method of knowledge; for in passivity the distinction between fact and illusion becomes meaningless because irrelevant to the demands of test.

What is more, the argument from surprise proves too much. Normally one feels no surprise over most of the experiences of the day. One expects the ice-cubes to mingle with scotch to the advantage of both. And if it is objected that one can't be sure the ice will melt and that every drink is a metaphysical surprise party, it becomes plain that one is arguing not from surprise to the transcendental origin of data, but rather from the postulated transcendental origin of data to the propriety or necessity of surprise when the matter has been soberly considered. And that is, of course, to beg the question. Or, would one argue that since the ice did melt as expected, and offered no surprise, that ice and coolness were no datum, and that a good drink was no more than an idea in the mind? The claim that every datum is a surprise is false; and that it ought to be a surprise begs the question.

Finally one may well regard the surprising datum as not at all objective, but rather as presumptively quite the opposite just because it clashes with expectations firmly established by one's view of nature. Indeed, what is too incoherently surprising becomes the antithesis of the objective.

In sum, surprise, where it occurs, marks the properties of subject as well as of object, and the absence of surprise entails no implication of the failure of objectivity, while its presence may suggest only error and illusion. Complete atomicity of data destroys surprise, subject, and object. The passive subject cannot define empiricism, but is rather its *reductio ad absurdum*. The passive subject is incapable of surprise.

III

It is also claimed that data are stubborn, and consequently bespeak their essential irrelevance to the subject. For it is supposed that one can do what one likes with mere ideas, while one is forced to surrender to the fiat of fact.

Probably no one any longer urges that there is no questioning of particular data; and whatever is to be understood by the stubbornness of data, it is not the Sinaiatic finality of one's belief that the tennis ball landed in. What is particular and accidental in data seems to be precisely what is not stubborn in them. Macbeth's dagger may proceed only from his heat-oppressed brain. The simplest observation, even of a sense quality, may turn out to be an hallucination. Data must make good before they can stand for fact, for what is more than mere idea. They are on trial; they must prove themselves.

On the other hand there are genuinely stubborn features of experience occurring in the psychological. For instance, there are beliefs, moods, conflicts, attitudes, which seem impervious to modification. Such accidents of personality are no more subject to voluntary change than are the accidents of perception. Indeed, it may well seem that men are stubborn, and intellectual content tentative and plastic. Yet this region of stubbornness is not the region of the non-psychological.

Statements about the self may be true or false; they are marked by the same tough insistence, by the same uncompromising independence as statements about the not-self. Stubbornness may show the region of truth; it does not imply that truth is independent of self, or concerned with the not-self. Stubbornness does not indicate irrelevance to the subject, and suggests no region separate from the subject; for it is also found in the subject.

It seems odd that so psychological an element as stubbornness should be used to differentiate the subjective from the objective. This is only a variation on those numerous attempts to denote the objective through its alleged subjective peculiarities; for example, that the perception of real objects is more clear, or more insistent, or more vivid than of the imaginary or hallucinatory. One can, of course, arbitrarily classify "true" content by such marks; but that is only to note differences within the psychological, and not a difference between the psychological and the impersonal. The basis of this distinction could not possibly be found in some peculiar property of psychological content. The distinction occurs only as a feature of the standpoint that defines the psychological in principle. But that standpoint will never disclose accidents as irrelevant to self, nor self as irrelevant to accidents.

The attempt to reach the impersonal or transcendent reality through logic has been abandoned wherever the relativity of logical order has been understood. It has been abandoned by anyone who has read Kant. But there persists the equally futile attempt to spin the real out of the psychological, and to find the evidence of the transcendental in some aspect of content. But neither the psychological nor the non-psychological can be discovered in content. This is Hume's correction of Berkeley's dogmatic assumption of the ego. Without content there is no subject and no object; but neither are they found in some peculiarity of content, such as stubbornness.

Besides the psychological, there is a further region of stubborn factors in experience, namely, in form and order. Form, lacking peculiar qualities, not being specific, occurring at no time or place, not red or sweet or cold, is not a casual apprehension of a subject. Even those who shrink from the *a priori* see in form a condition of specific perceptions. Perhaps those conditions represent to them only the helplessness of the ego, its prejudice or its animal faith, but a limitation nevertheless not to be transcended either by taking notice of nature or thought with oneself. Space, time, cause, quantity, relation, other self—these are indeed stubborn. What is more stubborn than the past? Yet the past is never as a whole, or in detail, a present content. It is not a datum, but a condition of data. The stubborn implies nothing transcendental or alien to the self, or to the structure of the point of view that receives particular accidents.

Finally, one may inquire into the status of assertions about data. If *they* are data, they are also irresponsible, catastrophic, changeable, and they require an inference from their catastrophe to their transcendental origin in order to show their own objectivity. But that is circular. Yet this consideration serves to disclose that the authority for arguing to the transcendental is not itself transcendental, but reveals the subject as the arbiter of reality. And if, on the other side, the assertions about data are not themselves data, we can only conclude that they revert to the subjective and thus lose all authority on the hypothesis of the argument.

In sum, the argument to the not-self on the basis of the stubbornness of data usually aims at no absolute certification of particular data, nor of what is accidental in data; it proves too much, since in both psychological attitudes and in formal order there reside exceedingly stubborn factors; and finally it can explain neither how statements about data are possible, nor how they could be true.

IV

To collect all data into a logical class and thereupon to regard that class as accidental to a prior situation seems impossible. "All" data, viewed as collected into a group, are not a possible object of experience. The concept of a class, legitimate for particular objects, becomes confused when applied to a formal condition of all objects. There is no class of all spatial objects, and no class of all qualified objects; for without space and without quality there are no objects. A true class need have no actual members, like the class of all centaurs, or of all passenger pigeons; but there is no point of view that can contemplate the absence of all data. It is no accident that there are accidents. *The concept of the accidental is not an accidental concept.* The point of view that asks about accidents is defined by their presence. And what defines the possibility of a question can never be treated as subject to question or to explanation. Yet to seek an explanation for the accidental is to treat it as unessential to the character of the real.

To explain the accidental it is necessary to presume a point of view free from it. And this point of view must thereupon find the accidental included in the absolutely determined, and thereby abolish the accidental. But the abolition of the accidental is the abolition of all order. It destroys the psychological, for the psychological functions express the limited, the exploratory, the novel. It destroys time. Accidents are the actuality of time. In the static order of scientific law there is no time because there is nothing unique and individual. Science furnishes laws of universal type which, while assuming individual events, describe the individuality of no event. In the scientific world there are no accidents, for science looks to the non-individual, ignoring the infinite extent of unique conditions out of which the timeless laws secure particular exemplification. The abolition of the accidental is the abolition of logic, for it destroys the tentativeness of assumptions which give inference its occasion and its force. Causal order is also lost, for cause, like all ideals, expresses a condition for the enlargement of unstable finitude and disappears with the limited point of view. In short, there is not one of the properties of order that fails to vanish with the abolition of the accidental.

The form of a world is an ideal, not an actuality, a framework for organizing and extending the accidental, and it disappears when accidents disappear. And so, the attempt to explain the accidental is essentially self-defeating, for all explanation is occasioned by accidents. Accidents account for the need of explanation, and to get rid of the accidental by invoking a prior situation where it plays no part is to make explanation meaningless.

For that reason, every philosophy that seeks to explain the accidental ends in a dogmatism, i.e., in realism. Fichte, for example, comes at last to a divine spirit whose ways are not our ways, whose meaning eludes all categories, and thus becomes an absolute not defined by what we define as thought. The same fate visits Royce and Bradley. This is not idealism. A *fait accompli,* even though called mental or spiritual, can be no factor in an idealistic metaphysics. For neither can it be made the object of a possible experience, nor could it possess experiences of its own.

The accidental is the actuality of the present moment, from which spreads the order of the world and its continuity through other moments. To recognize the present moment is to go beyond it, but one cannot get there before one arrives.* The dynamic of experience is an ingredient in its actuality, and the dynamic is the sole actuality of spirit, its work and its self-discovery. The modern world is not classic or Byzantine, where a dome of finality encloses finite perspectives. It is a surging world defined in its infinity, i.e., in its process of discovery; for any articulate infinite is only the articulation of the endeavor to know it. Thus the conception of the real meets the conception of the self, for they are the same fact viewed now focally in its dynamic, and now extensively in its objective potential.

Data in detail are psychological and personal, but the concept of the psychological is not a psychological concept. The psychological is not one of the accidents of experience, but defines its possibility. Consequently, the attempt to interpret the psychological status of data as a degradation to the subjective is a mistake. Again, the concept of the subjective is not a subjective concept. Data, i.e., accidents, are no more accidental in principle than is the psychological. It is true that metaphysics in its search for the real must escape the subjective; but this cannot mean that it must escape the subject. The order of appearances is reality, although not all appearances indicate the factual as against the fanciful.

Kant brought necessity into the accidental; what he did

*That anything should happen is necessary only if one starts with a happening. It isn't just the appearance or the idea which is finite; it is a situation, concrete, specific, and more or less grasped through symbols, depending on the degree of our clarity in dealing with nature.

not do, and what Hegel accomplished, was the bringing of the accidental into the necessary. This lesson has not been learned, even by most idealists.

The necessity of the accidental is a condition of form itself. Abstract form of any sort can get no illustration. One can give no idea of space without showing some; one needs to exhibit a particular piece of it, a piece made particular by content. And yet, because form is order, and order ideal, the given spatial fact moves outward toward the infinite in eternal contingency of every actual location. Order means contingency, and contingency touches no absolute terminal. This ideally infinite world shows the actuality and instancy of infinitude through the accidental. Because the accidental becomes intelligible only as it takes on form, it invokes the ideally endless extension of the finite for its own meaning, and thus attains order and explanation. At the same time it requires search into the conditions that produced it, thus generating ever new data and new problems. And in this expansion of explanation both form and content vindicate their own restlessness in the instancy of the real which they literally are, and of the life of which they are the substance and the activity. Accidents will happen where there is a world that can be understood. Only the accidental can challenge, and thereby occasion, understanding. The realistic error—and it is a systematically necessary error for the realistic procedure—is the attempt to explain the accidental as if it were itself an accident, one of the empirical peculiarities of experience rather than one of the conditions of experience. It is fair enough to require an explanation of every accident; it is meaningless to ask an explanation of the necessary. From this situation flows the curious instability of realism, its inability to make up its mind whether to be dogmatic or skeptical, and whether the dogmatic transcendental absolute is a God, or matter, or essences, or monads, or some combination of these. And so the skeptic appears, because the stage is set for him in advance by the dogmatisms resulting from the impossible task of explaining the accidental responsibly.

In sum, idealism has been strong in claiming for the

mind the order of experience, and weak in dealing with content. It has not, as a rule, made the accidental necessary. It has been abashed by arguments about surprise and about the stubborn character of data. Those arguments cannot define themselves without begging the question; for the absolute subject is nothing, and the absolute object is nothing. The accidental is an ontological concept, defining a condition of a world, and of a lawful world. Only in this lawful infinity can freedom be found or the secular become sacred.

4

On the Problem of Knowledge

The problem of knowledge occurs because of a distinction between appearance and reality, or thought and reality, or the psychological and the non-psychological. The problem takes the form of joining these two factors somehow.

The danger is that the problem will be abolished by rejecting one of the factors which occur in its meaning. Thus there is the danger of Berkeley's solution, where appearance becomes the same as reality. Berkeley does not want appearance to be regarded as *inadequate* to reality, or seem *different* from reality. He denies the reality which appears. Nothing appears. There is only appearance, and no question about appearance can be defined. He does not *solve* the problem, he *abolishes* it. *Appearance has no object.* Knowledge is not understood as the ground in appearance of something which does not and cannot appear. But where there is no quest there is no knowledge and certainly no problem. And, I would say, where there is no problem of knowledge there is *no knowledge*. For knowledge *means* the answer to a problem concerning the relation of appearance—or thought—to the real or the true. To know is not to have appearances; it is to validate and trust appearances. And where there is no question of such trust or mistrust, there is no meaning to knowledge. Any rejection of the factor of experience or of thought equally abolishes knowledge. That is all the same. The idea of knowledge is an idea of *self-consciousness*, i.e., of the place and role of appearance

as other than the self. The very idea of knowledge is, therefore, reflective. Berkeley lacked that control of his problem.

The two factors must be separate and they must be
joined. Objective idealism, generated from the position of
Kant, did join these. But its result was an absolute object
with no place for appearance. This absolute object was defined as thought. It was more than Berkeley's appearance. It
was *appearance plus order*. Appearance was no longer the
same as reality. *To be* was *to be thought,* not just perceived.
In fact, where to *be* meant to *be thought,"* appearance necessarily becomes only an episode. For thought defined law,
and law order, and order an infinite region incapable of
being perceived in any impression or through any sensation.

Appearances, once subjective, now become events in the
order of nature. To *thought* appearance is accident. It is the
framework of thought which alone gives to appearance the
status of the accidental. The order which surrounds them,
which produces them, gives them a non-subjective status.
They are in the rational order. Yet order implies none of
the particular appearances. Space does not imply the length
of Lake Seneca. So a strange *transposition* occurs in the status
of data or accidents. Radical empiricism (Hume) could ask
no questions about them, but Kant must ask questions.
Kant did not, of course, have a good answer. What he really
showed was the old distinction of reason (form) and psychology (data). That is all that Kant has to say, formally
considered. Still, the phenomenal had a unity in Kant. It
was "nature," where the particulars took place according to
a law. This law could not *generate* them, nor they the law.
Yet, disregarding the noumenal sources of form and of
control, there emerged a remarkable self-contained region
of nature where content always fitted into form. This phenomenal nature was *thought,* but it was *not appearance*. It was
a union of pure reason (form) and pure psychology (control). Thus its position *owed nothing to existence or to actuality*. It invoked no existent in its guesses, and produced
none in its sequel. The ontological proof was invalid.

This *region* of appearance I called an "object." Perhaps that is not accurate. But I called it that because it was not *appearance.* It was not psychological. It went its own way apart from what anyone might think because it stood for thought itself. Opinion could not modify it. Logic could only fortify it by repeating its structure. It was thought itself, and so attained independence of question, of what one might suppose. It had the finality of object, not the tentativeness of a subject.

Once more the essential of Berkeley's position occurs. Berkeley could not pass beyond appearance. Kant could *not pass beyond thought.*

The problem of knowledge requires the separation of the subject from the object. The subject tries to appropriate the object in order to check its own beliefs or impressions. There must be some factor of experience which invites that check, some factor which thought—or subject—must *keep on trying* to appropriate. The appropriation may never be complete, just as it may never be wholly frustrated. There must be systematic inadequacy in the subject, yet one which it can overcome.

What, then, is there to be overcome in the position of absolute idealism? There is, of course, ignorance, But all cases of ignorance get settled on terms known in advance. There is also error, but all cases get settled through logical modes also known in advance.

Thus thought works only within itself. But in principle it then has no opponent. The standpoint of natural knowledge becomes absolute. And that is always the standpoint of object-knowledge.

Idealism in Berkeley knows only impressions or ideas. In Kant and some of his successors, there is only *object* or *objects.* What is known is never thought, never *subject.* Kant, at least in the *Critique of Pure Reason,* offers only nature or object. Thought becomes equated with the object. The object is not countered by the subject, nor the subject by an object. That is the meaning of the statement that thought works only within itself in this picture. Its world lies before it. It has no antagonist.

(Of course in Kant the antagonist turned up as the noumenal. But that could never be captured. Still it goes to
show that thought was even here in need of its object, the
true, or the real.)

Now, while thought must have its object or antagonist
in order to pose the problem of knowledge, it is also the
case that the object must be defined in some relation to
thought. Otherwise one finds the problem insoluble because of the inherently alien character of the object of
thought. It must be object, but it must also be capable of
comprehension.

Well, at this point one has reached a crisis. Thought must
be the universal; yet, as knowledge, it must have an object
which it seeks.

There is a minor consideration here which has some interest. Thought is always as its object is. For example, Kant
had said that the unity of thought was the unity of its object, nature. The portrait of thought is in its object. But in
Kant's picture there is no original of the portrait. Nature is
there, and it becomes thought. Yet, looking at nature one
finds only objects. *One finds no subject,* no thinker, no
thinking. All that has been omitted. The original of the
portrait never turns up. Yet, nature is said to be a faithful
portrait. How does one know?

This is the twilight zone of absolute idealism. Neither
has thought an object nor has it a subject. Thought has
ceased to have a quest, and so has ceased to be true or even
false.

If thought seeks an object it seems plain enough that it
can leave it. All the destinations of experience are matters of
reflection, and all the particulars are matters of psychology.
Thought can own its world *as object.* Every unknown in
that region, every puzzling incoherence can be appropri-
ated because its status or incoherence derives only from
thought itself. Still, that leaves out the original of the portrait.

It would seem, then, that *to preserve the problem of knowledge* thought must become an object. It must do *more than
infuse or pervade* objects. It must be more than form. It must
be substance and actuality. Form and content are not suf-

ficient for actuality or for reality. They are only the *guise* of reality, its appearance and reason, not what appears, or has reason, or is *manifested* as appearance and as reason.

That thought must find the subject as well as the object is a condition for preserving the problem of knowledge. That consideration is the only control which I have used. It is the only one which can be used. In the theory of knowledge one has only the problem of knowledge. Anything more is dogmatic and question-begging. The answer to the problem can only be the meaning of the problem. *Neither appearance nor reason* can be the truth. These offer no problem to thought because they define it.

I think I have stated the problem about as well as I can especially in brief compass. The answer would require at least as long a treatment. But perhaps a suggestion would serve.

First off, one can't expect to find the original of thought as an object, i.e., as *one among the objects of nature.* The very function of natural knowledge is to make clear the form and order of *objects*.

Second, one won't find the original as subject considered *apart* from objects. Truth is not in subjectivity. Such a course would lead back to appearance. And a subject as the polar opposite of nature would be only a ghost. It is in nature that all concreteness and all articulation of thought, or of subjectivity, are found.

This narrows the field. What one needs to discover is an object, or *an aspect of object,* which is *not comprehended among the events of nature.*

I borrow now from Hegel and from Royce. The easiest approach comes from Royce, I think. It is his doctrine of "signs." I would prefer to use the word "symbol." A symbol is an object. A yardstick, a spoken word. These words are all objects. But they are objects which *nature cannot produce.* They are "expressive." They are objectified thought. They lead to the original of the portrait.

Perhaps this would be clearer if it were pointed out that Kant was quite wrong to present nature as a combination of psychology and reason. There is no such experience. Nature is thought about through symbols. *Destroy the symbol and one loses nature.* I mean destroy yardsticks, clocks, balances; destroy names and words, written numbers and logical notation, works of art and political constitutions, and nature reverts to chaos.

The symbol intervenes between subject and object and is directed toward both. These considerations lead to a theory of language. That this is in point you can see from the current efforts to reduce language itself to an object, to a part of the same order as sticks and stones.

The symbol generates nature. Act, not just thought, appears as a condition of truth. Nature is the portrait of which action is the original. Pure knowledge (mathematics, for example) is also pure act, the general form of action. To calculate is to use stones (calx). Very concrete, all that. Science is the form *and* the reality of pure act, of learning which rests only in the demand that there be a world for thought and practice. What one studies there is something *done*. The old stimulus-response psychology does not describe science. What a mistake to present *any* learning as response to objects in nature! All learning is *response to a response,* to an object which combines nature *and* self, objectivity and subjectivity. Only so can one go *wrong,* make mistakes, have error or tragedy.

We must abandon the whole business of a dyadic form of knowledge problem, i.e., the subject *versus* the object form. That will never provide the check to the subjective nor the objective which is more than an idea. Nor is a monistic solution any good. One needs a triadic relation, as Royce urged. There the real and true are original, but partial. One can seek their fuller meaning, but not their radically remote reality.

Some objects are a condition of knowledge. Such are symbols and the body. The "object of knowledge" must be defined through these objects which have consequences and generative capacity. Let's say that Lake Seneca is the object of knowledge, let's ask how long it is, or what its temperature is, or its elevation above sea level. One gets out the

yardstick, the thermometer, the barometer. There is something phony in the idea of knowledge when it gets presented as psychology or as pure form.

Symbols, in this case the instruments of physics, are
curiously apart from nature. Nature stays put while I get
out the yardstick. The roads lie still while I read the map
and move it closer to the light. Yet symbols are objects
too. But they are generative and critical. They stand for
thought, but not for the "object of thought" apropos of
symbols or instruments, not apropos of my psychology or
logic. That way it is only a mirage. It is time that one spoke
out and denied bluntly that one perceives an *object*. One
does not. One perceives nothing at all until existence and
actuality have been located and asserted as the *occasion* of
knowledge. So one asserts that ten paces forward is the
brook or the tree. But the ten paces are not an object ana-
lagous to the tree. They are an actuality, a reality giving rise
to knowledge of the tree. Knowledge of the tree is not
something that qualifies a subjective appearance of the tree.
It is something that develops from the reality of my position next to this boulder.

Russell and others have mentioned "knowledge about"
and "acquaintance with" as two forms of knowledge the
latter more direct, the former inferential. But I am not
proposing that I am "acquainted with" yardsticks or this
pen. In principle, *immediacy* must be present if there is to be
knowledge. That immediacy is *not treated as knowledge,*
especially not in its refined forms as instruments and symbols. I don't *know* that this is a yardstick; I *say* it is in order
to know how long a lake is Seneca. One can't question the
conditions of knowledge. In sum, knowledge is not, as
usually supposed, the attribute of an idea; it is the extension
of an actuality.

Put the real at the start and you have it in the end. Keep it
out of the beginning, out of the story of how any question
concerning what is true can be raised, and it will never turn
up at the end.

I challenge the view that there is thought without symbol and actuality. I deny that there is a region of reason and

of nature as mere essence, thought, or reason. Kant was dead wrong. So are all realists who ask about the "referent" of an idea. No idea can be articulated until peace has been made with actuality. There is no pure subjectivity; no pure objectivity. There is no question possible about the "truth" of what is only "idea" cut off from reality.

5

Idealism and Freedom

I

Idealism occurred historically as the outcome of the attempt to mediate between skepticism and dogmatism. This attempt finds its modern beginning in Kant. Hume had aroused him from his dogmatic slumber. How did this come about? Why should Hume have had the power to awaken the tranquil dogmatist?

It occurred because Hume had denied necessity. This was equivalent to the denial that any aspect of consciousness could be more than accidental. All experience derived from "impressions." Every impression could be some other way. Between impressions there were no connections capable of enforcing consequences. Any impression could follow any other. Among impressions there was no unity, actual or ideal. Nor was there any unitary self, or soul, as the central recipient of impressions. Berkeley had already stated that there was no "idea" of the soul; Hume now added that there was no "impression" of the soul and, by implication, no "notion" of it. He allowed unity neither in objects nor in the self. Atomic impressions were the sole data of expereince, and experience was confined to data.

Such a claim attacked dogmatism at its root. Dogmatism had asserted existences and unities which experience did not contain and which it could never certify. Thus, matter, soul, God, causality, logical order, obligation were not content of consciousness. They were either objects beyond all actual and possible experience, or else alleged universal laws of experience. Where all experience was confined to "impressions" there could occur to it neither such transcendent objects nor any such universal laws.

By Hume's time induction or empiricism had acquired great prestige. The scientific method was winning great victories. The naturalism of the eighteenth century was, however, still dogmatic. The causal argument was still used to establish both the rational order of nature and the existence of God as the author of nature. Hume's position was not that of the empirical naturalist. The naturalist was dogmatic both in his assumption of a logical order among the objects of nature, and in his conclusions based thereon. This vast structure Hume struck down. He did this by undermining its rationalistic foundations, namely the universal laws which both organized experience and then permitted the transition from nature to God.

Kant took seriously this reduction of all experience to the stream of consciousness. Himself something of a scientist, he had the scientific conscience. He believed that all statements about the content, or objects, of experience must be inductive. He saw that induction alone could generate no universal. Empirical procedure could not, he held, make verifiable or even meaningful statements about transcendent objects. Those two factors in traditional philosophy could get no support from an empirical method.

So far Kant went along with Hume. By doing so he abandoned dogmatism.

But Hume had destroyed more than dogmatism. He had also destroyed empiricism. At that point Kant balked.

To be empirical, said Kant, is to judge. Empiricism, as he saw it, was not the total absence of criticism. It was rather the restriction of criticism to the accidental, to impressions, to the content of consciousness. So much the psychological movement had made clear. But concerning that passively received psychological content, Kant differed from Hume, alleging that it always exhibited elements of organization, or of form. By denying form, Hume had made empiricism impossible. However correct Hume may have been in restricting knowledge to impressions, he was wrong, according to Kant, in supposing that those impressions were vagrant, unrelated, and without unity.

In proposing the categories as the form of impressions Kant was not repudiating empiricism. He was seeking, rather, to establish it. In effect, Hume had denied the possibility of judgment, since judgment entails compulsion. Without compulsion empiricism is reduced to indeterminism. Hume had made definition impossible because he had made all things possible, and definition means the rejection of some possibilities.

II

By this stroke of accepting empiricism while insisting on formal order Kant presented a new idea of first importance for the history of philosophy. It was that quite within the domain of thought itself there lay responsibility. Thought could police itself. Nature lost its status of opposition to thought, and became the ideal or theoretical meaning of any given perception, the extrapolation of the inherent form of any datum. The order of nature became the same as the order of judgment, or of criticism.

Both skepticism and dogmatism deny the self-limiting capacity of thought. The skeptic rejects the possibility of an alien control and finds none within himself. The dogmatist likewise finds no inner regulation, yet asserts a control exercised by laws or objects independent of thought. Both deny the autonomous authority of criticism. In the view of Kant, it was possible to stay within the confines of experience and still be critical. One could be mistaken. One could be limited and incomplete because of the formal order and the infinite relativity of thought itself. One needed to be faithful to the lawful form of one's own experience. In contrast to skepticism and dogmatism, thought was given power over itself. To have such power was its nature, a power inherent in every datum or impression.

A frequent misunderstanding of the Kantian position occurs in the charge that it is subjectivism. On this point Kant is clear. It is true that the criticism of appearances occurred solely through the operation of ideal form, and not through an appeal to laws, or to objects separate from the content to be criticized. This was not however the reduction of all thought to psychology. It was rather a claim that not all components of thought, or of experience, could be found in psychology. He urged a non-psychological aspect of experience, namely form, something not sensory, not accidental, not biographical. While unintelligible apart from content, it remained wholly ideal, the structure of content, its law, and its organized pattern. In this way accidental content became at once limited in fact and, at the same time, infinite in its ordered relations. Limitation was combined with infinity through the law. Empirical statements became also responsible statements. Subjectivism is not the view that all experience possesses a lawful and ideal form; it is rather the view that all experience, being only psychological, lacks such lawful form. From the standpoint of psychology there are no universals. Kant asserted universals by denying the claim of psychology as the exhaustive account of experience. His claim was this: no experience without law, a law inherent to experience itself. The factor in Kant's position which has often been an obstacle to philosophers is just this presentation of a non-psychological element in empiricism. This is his resolution of the conflict between an atomic empiricism devoid of formal limitation, and a dogmatic assurance devoid of the limitation of accidental content.

The charge that Kant was a subjectivist is too weak to warrant much consideration. A much stronger charge is that he was not subjective enough. He spoke of his phenomenal world as "consciousness in principle." Yet, consciousness occurs only in the individual. Kant left obscure the place of quite personal experience in his highly impersonal account of nature. One may doubt whether idealism has been clear on this point, especially in its more popular versions. Idealism has been tolerably successful in claiming ideality for law; it has not been equally successful in relating

that law to biography and to history. Its characteristic difficulty occurs in its omission of individuality and finitude,
rather than in an exaggeration of the personal stream of
consciousness. It was for this reason among others, that
James objected to Royce's Absolute, and Royce himself
saw the need of avoiding the obliteration of the individual
in the world. It would seem that the usual charge against
idealism is not subjectivism, but rationalism, its tendency
to eventuate in some dogmatic completion. Idealism, it is
often held, slights the factor of the accidental, of the finite,
of the non-rational. Schopenhauer found that fault with
Hegel, while James urged a pluralistic universe and a finite
God. Of course, there are many philosophies other than
idealism which attempt to "explain" the finite and the accidental by treating them as properties of appearance, but
not ultimately of the real. All such "explanations" of the accidental are necessarily dogmatic. The agnostic element in
Kant registers his recognition of this result.

III

Idealism after Kant consists in the discovery and exploita-
tion of the non-psychological factors of experience. They
are the factors of structure, and consequently of criticism,
for criticism is nothing other than the self-maintenance of
structure. It seems tolerable to assume that the denial of
structure is all the same as the denial of criticism. It seems
equally persuasive that the authority of criticism depends
on the necessity of those structures in accordance with
which criticism operates. Let it be urged that the modes of
criticism lack equivalence with the real, and it follows that
authority itself is only appearance, animal faith perhaps, or a
convenient code for getting a little order out of the mess of
running experience.

The sticking point in the understanding of post-Kantian
idealism is precisely this claim that structure is absolute. It
seems clear that no absolute can secure logical demon-
stration. There can surely be no point of view which could

ever *certify* the pretension of necessity. And we are accustomed to suppose that what has no environment is the very essence of the arbitrary.

The idea of statements having no environment is not, however, totally unfamiliar. The scientific honesty of our time has scrupulously explored those elements of knowledge which are asserted without evidence. Especially has this been the case in logic, mathematics, and physics. There one encounters the "postulate" in all its underived primitiveness. Granting disputes over the precise postulates of any one of these areas of orderly study, still it seems agreed by all hands that what allows order and responsibility is some such list of unverifiable assertions. All postulates refer to order and its elements. None refers to particulars.

An unverifiable assertion, since it is about nothing in particular, is a very peculiar idea. Assertions about particulars are contingent. They owe their meaning, and their contingency, to the sort of organization which identifies specific situations. They are not about structure, for structure is neutral to all possible particulars. This state of affairs has given the positivists their inning. Assertions about nothing in particular, they say, make no sense. Since no assertion can secure verification apart from particular differences, it is obvious that wholly formal statements are, for positivism, without meaning.

Nevertheless, from the beginning of philosophy there has been a search for these "organization words." Words having denotation have seemed not to concern philosophers. But what authority have organization words? Indeed, what is the peculiar urgency which invents so perverse an idea? At any rate, their authority and their meaning must be related to that urgency. Their authority will depend on the absoluteness of that urgency.

IV

No one will be in accord with an answer to a question unless he accepts the validity of a problem. And, certainly, no answer can be viewed as necessary where the problem is believed to be accidental or gratuitous. At the same time, neither can an answer be accepted as necessary when the problem has an environment apropos of which it occurs. The foundations of thought, and the character of reality, would then, of course, revert to the scheme of that environment. Consequently, any problem about reality must be identical with reality. The problem must be unconditioned if it is to convey an unconditioned answer.

Instead, then, of proposing the unconditioned as an answer let it be considered as the property of a problem. This would be a problem about structure, for it is only in structure that thought shows its authority. Only in a problem about structure could this authority be seen in its urgency and in its origin.

A problem marks disconcertment. It is the claim of idealism that some disconcertments are constitutional, not accidental. They occur as a threat to control, not to a detail within controlling law. Incoherence of a radical sort means a systematic inability to deal with particulars, a confusion of procedure. It threatens thought itself. By the same token it threatens nature itself, for the order of nature accepted at any historical period reflects the modes of making sense out of experience.

This threat to thought must, of course, turn up within thought. It occurs as conflict, the conflict of unreconciled demands of modes of apprehension. Accordingly, the origin of Western philosophy records the first self-conscious conflict. It was the problem of change. Events without unity made no sense. It was not until Plato's *Parmenides* that we received a document delicately aware that the ideal of complete unity would be no less frustrating than absolute variety. The history of philosophy is the record of such necessary conflicts.

They are necessary because only in them is the presence of thought revealed. It seems plain that thought as "consciousness" has never been given a clean bill of health. Consciousness remains hidden, or else one finds it reduced to unconscious nature. It is only in self-consciousness that thought draws its own portrait. If it is possible to know thought it could be only by means of itself. Yet were thought "consciousness" it would be, as it has been, elusive, not capable of distinguishing between itself and nature. That was the position, and it is the meaning, of Berkeley. For Berkeley anticipated Hume in holding all "ideas" passive and hence without structure. The mind, or soul, alone was action, he believed, and for that reason could not show itself. Since what did show itself was only idea, the soul remained in Berkeley a dogmatic residuum. Allegedly active, its activity was recondite, never mirrored in the very content of consciousness.

It was Hegel who undertook a systematic study of conflicts. They are the phenomenology of the spirit, the modes of thought's reality and self-consciousness. The solution of any conflict, or rather its resolution, lies in realizing the necessity of the conflict. Each factor is high lighted by its antagonist, disclosing its imperative role only to the degree that it meets frustration. Consequently, each factor has a stake in its antagonist.

For example, "purpose" has a stake in "cause." No purpose can define itself, nor can it secure execution, apart from the order of nature. Similarly, cause has a stake in purpose. No cause can be discovered in passivity and none can be demonstrated without experimental control. Each needs the other, and thought needs both. In its concreteness, an event in nature appeals elliptically to the purpose or the act by which it secures organization.

Consider the position of skepticism as a further illustration. The skeptic denies affirmation. The verb "to be" equals the verb "to seem." Yet, skepticism must live in a haunted house, forever invoking the ghost of nature as the means of securing its own vivid isolation. It is haunted by its denial. At the same time, skepticism is the very position which thought must first take in order to distinguish itself from nature. It is the systematic and necessary discovery of the omnipresence of thought. No one can be a philosopher who has failed to experience the force of skepticism. Dogmatism is only the illegitimate escape from skepticism, a very common procedure. Until thought finds its own features in its antagonist, dogmatism and skepticism remain the two unavoidable basic philosophies, although their forms be protean.

These conflicts bring out the factors of structure in discourse. They indicate the ways of thought, and hence the elements of organization and of criticism. They are the evidence of responsibility because the vehicles of threat to one's own coherence. They have no imperative except that of one's own self-assertion. One cannot induce anyone to accept such conflicts. They reveal their imperative quality only because they cannot be induced in others. It seems plain that no one can feel as his own predicament what his very self does not propose and demand. The practice of teaching philosophy by argument is widespread. But any such procedure is the plainest evidence that nothing necessary can result. The quality of philosophy is not strained. Its authority and compulsion must wait upon each person's acknowledgment of his own identity with its problems. Its force is derived from the discovery that all compulsion occurs as the demand of some aspect of organization. The willingness to assume risks of disorder for the sake of allowing imperatives to make themselves clear is the mark of the philosophic spirit. There is no conventional philosophy, but only the free discovery by the individual of his own reality through a wholly free activity.

Consequently, the progress of philosophy must wait upon historical events. As we build lives and states upon some view of order, we let loose upon ourselves the consequences of any flaw in that view. If a man's world runs smoothly he can have no philosophic problems. Only as events with which he has identified himself and his hopes threaten his own outlook with destruction can he begin to take stock. This is the rationale of the comic and the tragic.

V

In politics we are today struggling to secure free institutions. But it is obvious that, to use a phrase of Walt Whitman's, we have no "metaphysics of democracy." Indeed our currently successful doctrines repudiate metaphysics, alleging that democracy is the triumph over such fantasies.

Yet even the democratic man must have dignity. Sovereignty, whether monarchial or democratic, needs sanction. This sanction turns on the responsibility of the sovereign, and on reverence for his pronouncements. One does not escape tyranny by multiplying irresponsible and subjective arbitrariness. Every man may be a king; but in our time a king must be a constitutional authority. He must carry responsibility in his person. It is a great illusion to suppose that government will protect rights when actual individuals display nothing but desires in their wills, and nothing but opinions in their minds. Such doctrines paralyze resolve. They are degenerate, and they invite the conqueror and the despot. What shows men to be free is their capacity to recognize and revise the grounds of their choices and of their opinions.

There is just one quality in every man which he must change at least once; he must change his philosophy. Only in the discovery of some fatal threat to himself in the framework of his inheritance can he discover freedom. There alone does he confront a necessary and an absolute problem, one proposed by himself and suffered in himself. Freedom is not, as so many have said, in choice; it is rather the revision of the basis of choice. What a man chooses, what he believes, can easily be reduced to psychology and to circumstance. But the complex structure through which choice occurs can never be. Psychologists know this. That is why psychology denies meaning to the universal and the critical.

Philosophy must join men of action, the history makers. But philosophy is too ancient and too informed to suppose that history is made by the moralists or the purveyors of circuses. It is made by those who have not shrunk from the conflicts which challenge a present outlook, who have seen those conflicts through in physics and in politics. Those conflicts are the phenomenology of the spirit, the stations of its career, the secular stations in the cross. It is this story which is both history and philosophy. Argument saves a man from himself, from the ultimate loneliness where he finds his freedom. Argument is never fatal. It makes no history. But philosophy is the actuality of those conflicts which establish the grounds upon which arguments occur and by which they are regulated. That lies beyond argument and proof. It is the career of the self-conscious and the generation of outlooks.

This, I suggest, is the base of a philosophy of freedom. This is the only universal common to all minds. One need respect no man because he eats and drinks. One is not compelled by his psychology. But one must be concerned with him in so far as he stands forward as one who has come to himself, and through his conflicts has paid the price.

Politically, the future will be oriented on the problem of winning power for each man. This is not power over nature, but power of one man over another, and every other. But power of that sort can never be physically enforced. It must proceed from respect. And respect can be bought only at the price of that inner conflict through which a man's life becomes the forfeit of his truth.

What Kant proposed was the capacity of thought to police itself. He did not carry out that idea. Since then it has grown. Since then the idea of history has been brought into the open. History is the order of the unique. It declares the efficacy of time in the meaning of events. Physics and logic do not do this. History is the vindication of inwardness, the record of its daring and of its transforming victories. The idealism of the future will be a philosophy of history, of action, of a self-generating, lawful finitude. Such are the conditions of a metaphysics of democracy.

6

History and Humanism

The idea of a philosophy of history may, at first sight, seem contradictory. History is of all subjects the most earth-bound and time-bound, not venturing beyond the records and documents which set forth what has happened in a particular place and time. Philosophy has, from the first, been concerned with eternal objects rather than with events in time. Philosophers will often consider a proposal as if it possessed meaning anywhere, and at any time. One may seriously debate the problem of mind-body dualism, as if it were a question of general concern, touching all men everywhere. Not uncommonly, the doctrines of the great figures in the history of philosophy are presented in this way. Such treatment of men and issues creates an atmosphere to which time and accident seem irrelevant.

Furthermore, there are in fact many philosophies which set out to proclaim a doctrine of salvation, which is to be found precisely in the measure that one can identify oneself with truths and values which rust and moths cannot corrupt. Perhaps those attempts may be regarded by some as poor doctrine, but they cannot be disavowed. And they represent that quest for imperturbability, for stoutness in the face of fortune, which is commonly associated with the name of philosophy.

If one seeks eternal truth one may perhaps inquire of the philosopher, but hardly of the historian. Historians deal in the transitory and corruptible. They have no interest in any event or statement except so far as it falls within time and is accounted for by other quite temporal events in accordance with methods of interpretation which are themselves but changing fashions. Of this strange involution of his work the historian is often subtly or even explicitly aware. He works in a field that has its own infinity, but it seems a shapeless one. Everything that gets done by an act is grist for his mill. There seems no solid ground under his feet. He cannot even indulge in the luxury of philosophic skepticism, for that position registers defeat in the quest of an ideal which the historian does not seek, and which he must treat like all else as another hope or expression of belief.

Looked at this way, history is a study which appears to dissolve the solidity of nature into opinions about nature, and to treat the most elaborate scientific studies of objective reality as no more than human documents. For traditional philosophy, i.e., for philosophy that is itself ahistoric, such a study can have no form because it has no controls. It is a Humean essay where the data include the tentative organizations which are acts, and the symbols which acts leave as their residue. But if one asks for the fixed frame of reference in which this discourse operates there appears to be none, and none seems possible. For were one proposed, the acts, events and symbols which history studies would fall into that ahistoric frame of reference and time would be lost in the static.

For this reason history seems to be a study without form. And if it has a form it must be a new one, construed out of the elements of change, time, and finitude. Time and history can have no form except that of time itself. To see whether that is possible is one way of posing the idea of a philosophy of history.

The idea of a "philosophy of" does not fall in too readily with this situation. To undertake a "philosophy of" some special science is to seek to identify, analyze, and relate the categories in which it operates. For example, minimal elements in mathematics are the factors of identity and difference, pure and abstract, and without qualification of space, time, or sense property. These factors are universals and they are taken to hold sway anywhere and at all times. They are concepts of universal incidence, organization words, not denotation words. They seem general conditions of all discourse. And they are therefore treated as being timeless. They are eternal essences. So, too, when in physics the list of categories expands to include space, time, and body there is no suggestion of any local event, of anything that happens in a particular place and time. Such a pattern for the idea of history is inappropriate. A philosophy of history must be a story in terms of time, and of events in time. In history there is no static truth antecedent to its own investigations.

It may be felt that tentativeness and insecurity mark all sciences, including philosophy, and that all beliefs suffer change. This may very well be the case but for all that it does not make for clarity in defining this issue to obscure the aim of a study. It seems most likely that all persons feel the attraction of history's absolute empiricism, but this does not imply that philosophy has usually regarded itself as nothing but history, or its quest confined to events in time. On the contrary, I believe, philosophy has not widely announced that finitude is a category, i.e., a constituent factor of the real. On the whole, philosophy has sought the ahistoric, with realities and forces which deny efficacy to time, and leave it in a region of shadow.

Time has been a cosmic step-child of dubious parentage, and always a problem child. It is commonly represented as moving in bad company with ignorance, impulse, and vice. It is the scene of our fall from the true and the good, our alienation from the ideals of knowledge and virtue. The problems of error and of evil are among the most common in philosophy.

Philosophy has proposed that we become the spectators of all time and all existence. All things are to be viewed under the aspect of eternity where if one must love God, it is to be done intellectually, and not from a passionate heart. There have been first causes, prime movers, unmoved movers, substances both one and many and of every description, atoms and their prolific progeny, or laws through which the bewildering changes of time might be arranged in patterns of unvarying constancy. But everywhere time is a doom, an exclusion from the ideal. It is finitude, a region in which philosophy has not characteristically found rest and sufficiency of being.

It may be felt that time is quite an acceptable concept since it occurs in physics. But the time of physics differs in important ways from the time of history. In physics time has no efficacy. There, no event is understood because of yesterday, but only because it illustrates the dateless law. For this reason it deals in the repeatable and therefore permits experiment and observation, neither of which procedures operates in history. The experiment has a date, but not the order of nature which it is designed to reveal. The laws of moving bodies hold no less today than yesterday, and as surely in Poonah as in Pisa. Physics has become a very paragon of knowledge and enjoys enormous prestige. But it purchases this sublimity at the price of a radical impersonality and at least an apparent irrelevance to action and values, a feature of impersonal knowledge which has proved disturbing to humanists. Physics defines a region without blemish, a seamless garment of nature. It contains no error, no passion, no evil, and no conflict. Facing it men may abandon hate, but will not, as some seem to suppose, find love. It remains ahistoric in all its immensity, and somberly threatens to disqualify limitation and all those areas of experience which must give to limit a central and controlling function.

In survey: to deny ontological status to finitude is to disqualify historical time, and yet to give time the status of a category appears to bar access to that totality of object and integrity of person which philosophy purports to offer.

There is about the concept of time the flavor of empiricism, i.e., the rejection of the complete. It is not to be assumed, however, that a defense of the systematic status of time and limit will win the approval of all empiricists. Indeed, the idea of history, since it carries us into the past which is irrevocable, is less agreeable to the usual versions of empirical knowledge than is the idea of the eternally contemporary. For there tests can be made, and the common and public world established. It seems possible to suppose that empiricism owes its continuing, as well as its original appeal, to its promise to unveil the impersonal and objective truth, the truth about nature which can be useful to men. Bacon took knowledge to be a kind of power, and our contemporary instrumentalists still inveigh against any concepts of truth which do not accrue to the execution of particular purposes.

Scientific empiricism has sometimes become positivism which, in extreme form, involves the repudiation of criticism. An outcome of this tendency has been logical positivism, where the form of finitude is lost in the description of a peculiar datum, namely language. The general position of incompleteness is threatened by empiricism with loss of form, and so with a loss of the necessary, i.e., metaphysics. It becomes difficult to avoid reduction of all beliefs and statements to psychology. This is the historic and characteristic charge made against empiricism.

The difficulties which occur in the study of a philosophy of history center on the disposition one makes of the element of limit. It seems plain that the problem of historical order would be most seriously affected by the assumption of antecedent determinism. It is a question of one's frame of reference, of how one would tell the story. One would certainly need to be very cautious about allowing history to vanish into some ahistoric background of which it would become only a phenomenal derivative. Nor would it in the least matter whether such a background turned out to be mundane or celestial. One can abandon all ontology, but what one cannot do is to define the ontological in some a-historic way and then propose a philosophy of history. Physics, psychology, or theology may well take over, but one should then raise no fundamental puzzles about the order of events in historical time.

There is a proper reluctance in the acceptance of any compulsive idea. And ontology is compulsive. The over-all quality of experience or of nature is not disclosed in any

event which could be some other way. It goes without saying that one does not want to make an *argument* for finality.
Whatever is proved is unsure, and whatever happens is
without constitutional force. To represent history as a category is to offer it as compulsive. One needs to discover
how that can be done.

There is a sentence in Descartes' *Discourse on Method*
which may serve as an indication for dealing with this
problem of compulsion as it relates to finitude. Descartes
wrote: "For it occurred to me that I should find more truth
in the reasonings of each individual *with reference to the affairs in which he is personally interested,* and the issues of
which *must presently punish him if he judged amiss,* than in
those conducted by a man of letters in his study, regarding
speculative matters that are of no practical moment, and
followed by no consequences to himself, farther, perhaps,
than that they foster his vanity the better the more remote
they are from the common sense; requiring, as they must
in that case, the exercise of greater ingenuity and art to
render them probable." What is here, I suggest, the important phrase is this: *"the issues of which must presently punish
him if he judged amiss."* This penalty, Descartes points out, is
not found among speculative matters. And yet Descartes
was not a pragmatist either, trying to find ways and means
of satisfying an accidental or instinctual want. His problem
of discovering a true method of knowledge will seem to
most persons speculative enough, yet it was apropos of
such a quest, deliberately remote from accidental particulars, that he spoke of being visited by some penalty for his
failure. Philosophy is viewed by many as a study without
consequences, i.e., as a study which cannot specify the
punishment for failure. The real difficulty, however,
occurs apropos of showing how failure could occur among
the universals, even a failure of reason; for there is no logic
among the essences. A practical failure, touching us in our
finitude and partiality, would hardly seem to make sense in
eternity.

One may well hold that any belief has consequences because it gives shape to personality and character and there-

fore controls action. This is often claimed. William James thought that "over-beliefs" bore upon one's hopes and fears, and so upon one's undertakings, and he identifies rationalist and empiricist as men of differing stamp. "See the exquisite contrast of temperaments," he exclaims. Fichte in *The Vocation of Man* admits himself stopped in persuasion by the character of materialists and idealists; and Plato in describing the career of various political types speaks of the democratic man or the timocratic man as responsible for the parallel forms of government. In his *Types of Philosophy* Professor Hocking quotes a remark of Chesterton's that "the most practical and important thing about a man is his view of the universe." Perhaps we can do nothing about the universe, but our view of the universe seems to do things to us and to others.

Descartes is not clear on the meaning of the punishment which follows error. But it seems fair to believe that he did not mean that one became ill, or lost one's money, or laid oneself open to a suit at law. The punishment was not, it seems, of the sort visited upon imprudence or ignorance of the ways of the world. In general, if the consequences of a philosophy are to be construed as practical the controlling concern of the individual would then fall into the particular satisfactions of life and not in the intrinsic fulfillment of philosophy itself. Somewhere, great satisfactions must be shadowed by a great threat. But what threat, what punishment, what nemesis is there among the categories and the eternal essences? They seem remote from consequences and have been traditionally courted for that very reason. And when they do have consequences they lose their priority and stand under the smiles and frowns of common pleasures.

Yet failure to discover punishment of a fundamental sort is likewise failure in the quest for the necessary ingredients of experience. So far as I can tell, the instrumentalist party in pragmatism cannot define radical failure, and consequently must repudiate all necessities. A view of truth based on purpose, i.e., on psychology, would not, of course, be able to name any fundamental threat.

The punishment of which Descartes speaks conveys the flavor of an inescapable consequence, as if there were something more operative than intelligence and circumspection. There is here a suggestion of darkness, of forces to which one must bow, of something restless and inescapable, while at the same time made operative and manifest *in time* and to finite endeavor. And it seems well to say again that the penalty in question does not frustrate an aim which is itself avoidable, an aim which one might relinquish without any sense of radical defeat or defect. College students sometimes consult psychologists who purport to tell them the occupation in which they might best hope to succeed. Should it turn out that a penchant for medicine gets no support through such an analysis, the young man may turn to law or business with no sense of defeat, and sometimes with a sense of satisfaction over the discovery that he can be more successful, or useful, in those endeavors. But here defeat is not fundamental. One turns to something else. There are other fish in the ocean. But a radical frustration presumes a radical aim. How are we to be punished in time for our metaphysical defects? Yet how else can punishment be administered? Were one to say that one cannot escape nature one would, I believe, find a broad tendency to agree. There has also been uttered the statement that we cannot escape history. This was said at a time of great emergency in the American career. Something was at stake, and this was declared to be the last best hope of earth. There was in prospect a new birth of freedom and the more secure establishment of the institutions which expressed and guarded the endeavor of men to achieve their befitting excellence. There was here a threat and a promise, the prospect of consequences of a grave and controlling sort.

There were many who *did* want to escape history, to exclude the inexorable from time. For while time is a doom from the point of view of eternity, it is an opportunity for those who mistrust responsibility and hope to elude nemesis. With this attitude, the attempt to escape from the shocks of necessity, one may have the deepest sympathy. Santayana makes much of the shock of data, and of the confusion and instability visited upon the soul in the entire region of action, the region of animal faith.

Others have sought to avoid the issues of essence by dwelling only in time and so making the best of circumstances. History, however, is satisfied with neither solution. Its peculiar flavor is found in the union of form and finitude, in the acceptance of time as a region from which one cannot escape because it is the condition of the disclosure of all necessities.

The residual heresy of the idea of history as it is of the idea of action and of morals is that we can very easily escape history by renouncing all egoism. So can we, on that basis, escape nature. For nature, I venture to say, is no datum. It is, perhaps, environment, but even as environment the extension of will. Nature, as order, is pure act. Physics is a study of the general conditions of action, and it is a science which has obtained scope and articulation only as egoism has sought out the general conditions for all particular purposes. It is this which bestows on physics its non-psychological quality while at the same time drawing it into the orbit of the humanities. We can escape nature, and we can escape history, and we will always try to do both in so far as we would shrink from that punishment of which Descartes spoke.

The terror which has been spread abroad by the atom bomb is the disclosure that many do shrink from nature and the awful power which it bestows on those who know its ways. But it also marks the point where physics enters history, not as an accumulation of knowledge, or the removal of ignorance, or the extension of means for the accomplishment of psychological purposes, but as an enterprise shrouded in fate and sustained by the dark forces of will. In the Old Testament there was an avoidance of the true name of the deity, and we confront a parallel reluctance to use the name of nature. How different this is from the optimism of Francis Bacon collecting "instances" the better to extend his power. Knowledge is not power; it is rather fate and the disclosure of the systematic relation of limit to essence. Knowledge is not the way to eternity; it is the way

to history. Until knowledge discloses its systematic penalty it dwells in its ivory tower or else becomes the ignoble
servant of arbitrary and subjective aims. The Baconian aim
has failed. It has become a nightmare and a menace. This is,
I believe, the reason for the bewildered and sincere cries
which demand that nature study be now bent to human and
to humane purposes. This effort too, will fail. There is
nothing we can do to escape from the perils which attend
our discovery of the necessary. For these perils are our fate,
and they alone give to fate any meaning. The fault may not
be in our stars, but in ourselves. But this does not make us
underlings. Nor does it make us masters. It leaves us
caught in a destiny of our own making, where every inexorable force represents one of the conditions of our own
finitude. *The absolute is the form of finitude.* This, so far as I
can see, it the simplest way of formulating the meaning of a
philosophy of history. The punishment of which Descartes
spoke is the consequence in time of the unwillingness to
treat time as a category. There is not, so far as I can tell, any
other way of bringing home to any man the experiential
equivalent of necessity.

No man will accept necessity until something happens to
him to make him do so. Yet this seems absurd, since what
happens is regarded as never necessary. We are not dogma-
tists, nor do we usually allege that we have stood on Pisgah
and seen the promised land. We must settle for experience,
yet experience being finite and fragmentary seems a most
unlikely source of the inescapable. It discloses no meaning
to punishment. Even the civic punishment of wrongdoers,
so-called, illustrates this hesitation. Ignorance of the good,
as Socrates urged, calls for instruction. There seems no
ground of punishment until the wrongdoer has fitted himself for it by accepting the equation between himself and
finitude. History is the maintenance of finitude, and more
closely, its self-maintenance. I suggest, in passing, that this
is the reason why Plato kept returning to the problem of
virtue, baffled by an inability to discover the locus of evil,
and of good, in limitation itself.

In broad summary: Philosophy has difficulty in including history where the past exerts efficacy and the static laws themselves dissolve into the fluidity of experience. But among the essences there is no necessity because no penalty. Descartes proposed such a penalty. How is one to interpret it as falling within experience? How is limit to contain anything unconditioned? Time confronts us at last with the constraints generated by egoism, i.e., by any assertion of the conditions of finite existence. These include nature and all knowledge. History is disclosed when any attempt whatsoever at assertion, whether theoretical or practical, forces upon us the sense of inherent fatality and compels attention to the self-maintaining process. It is apropos of this process alone that all necessity is disclosed and definable.

Against this background we can now move to name and briefly characterize some concepts and theories which are involved in a philosophy of history.

A remarkable and, I think, defining element in the generation of the historical process is the need of commitment. This is the mark of limit, and of self-identification with limit. In the more intellectual sort of historical development, skepticism may serve as an example. Skepticism is not an original position, but is always derivative. One may be born great, but one must achieve skepticism. It does not matter, however, in what naive belief doubt finds origin. It is only necessary that there shall have been a belief in something. Naturalism unexamined is as ready a medium for skeptical growth as supernaturalism, and just as inevitably a producer of misgivings. Skepticism is generated only by the formal fact that one has been committed to some belief or other, no matter what. It is a position perpetually regenerated as new knowledge becomes customary or hereditary. In skepticism there occurs the alienation of thought from its object, and so, in all times, the rediscovery of the solitude of thought itself. This transition does not, and cannot, occur where one is thoughtless, without a stake in some view of man's qualities or nature's order. Only the man with a theory, with some, perhaps unclear, universal belief, can suffer this disturbing disillusionment. Experience, when articulate and possessed of some formal order, however elementary or sophisticated, must pass down the road of self-discovery. One has trusted sense, or judgment, or revelation, tradition or reason. But somewhere one has given one's faith.

To show that all philosophical ideas emerge from the pressures of commitment could require prolonged exhibition in many types of philosophical study. For I do think it is at last a matter of exhibition, rather than of abstract argument. Still, the career of a commitment may be carried a step farther in considering the historic fate of skepticism itself. Being a product, it is itself transitional, an advertisement of limit and instability. Something more is called for. Perhaps one inspects this lonely self and finds that it veils a further unexamined assumption, perhaps that of a thinking substance. This, however, also vanishes into the phenomenal data, and one comes to the question of the radical empiricist, "Does consciousness exist?" Still, it is hard to ignore the base degrees by which one has risen to nonentity and annihilation. So long as any position is taken, even a denial, even the stream of consciousness, one still maintains some outlook, however desperate and impoverished.

This is the part of the record which thereupon produced the essay of Kant. It is always difficult in dealing with the history of philosophy to demonstrate that a figure in a standard textbook ought to be in the textbook. There are those who would stop the story with St. Thomas, and others favor John Locke, holding, with James, that philosophy goes around Kant, not through him. It is not simple to show just why Fichte, for example, belongs in the history of philosophy and why the position of nature received from him a treatment enforced by the commitments of his predecessors. But throughout one must, I believe, maintain this attitude of tension and desperation in order to keep one's discourse historical. Not every word spoken in philosophy can hope for such distinction.

It is, consequently, a great mistake to quarrel with the figures who make history. One does not stand outside the issues of philosophy and judge them. They are judged by history alone, i.e., by any successor who had embraced prior commitments, made them his own and suffered their bewilderment. If he thereupon accepts his task, maintains the validity of the problems which produced confusion, he may hope to add something to clarity. The philosopher, like the artist or statesman, must settle with some actual and self-defining difficulty and speak to its demands. One is entitled to suspect those reformers who see in the past the record of errors and confusions which might have been avoided in a fuller possession of ahistoric truth. For them there is no history but only static and intellectual truth.

In a broader sense, all history displays this equation between selfhood and actuality. This is the stage on which all action occurs. Action announces limit. Infinity cannot act, and speculation need not. In the present time we face great issues, greater and more searching than ever before in the history of our country. If we can find the actuality which is for us self-defining, and hence absolute, we shall know what to do. Otherwise we may well suffer disintegration and defeat. But what we are is what we have come from. There we find our necessary meaning, because there we find the meaning of our problems and of our finitude. From that process and its results we cannot escape.

I have felt that this idea of commitment, of an absolute, though finite actuality, exerts considerable appeal for young men, especially to those who have interposed their bodies and their wills between their country and its enemies. It seems to me shameless to suggest that the soldier faces destruction and deals it out, or that he could be asked to do so, for any but a final cause. And it seems to me no less inhuman to engage in these undertakings for theoretical ends. This is the locus of our confusion over the actual. We are intellectualists, we are spectators, and cannot therefore conceive of the absoluteness of limitation. This problem has become one of morale, and of our survival. We must beware of the suggestion that our wits are sharper, our theories surer than those of our enemies. We dare not allege that we have unveiled some abstract good, or essential vir-

tue, and now propose to use violence in order to make our
theories prevail. What we must preserve is not an abstract
ideal, but limitation and finitude. We must preserve history.

The only punishment is the loss of the capacity to make
history, to come to an end of a self-defining task in which
lies all compulsion and all universality. These are the reasons why we cannot escape history. This, rather than the
bare space of Plato, is the mother and nurse of all existence.
And in that medium of time is also the generation of all essence. For the universal is the form of limitation and in all
its modes declares the order of critical finitude.

A great deal of effort has been expended in avoiding
parochialism of both will and belief. Our loyalties, it is
urged, should embrace all mankind. Toynbee fears the
idolatry of local attachments. In one way or another this is a
familiar theme, and has often appeared in moral theory as
the ever-widening circle of membership. We aspire to become citizens of the world and to embrace all men in good
will. Yet the good will must also interpret itself in specific
ways. No good can be accomplished where specific institutions and commitments do not shelter its growth and foster
its exercise. We may well shrink from such localism. It
seems to destroy, not to promote, the universal. Yet a corollary of the possibility of history occurs in the necessity of
asserting the absoluteness of some actual embodiment of
values. If this is narrowness and idolatry, it is also loyalty,
and the condition of affection. That morality occurs in limit
and only there, that it is not the reaching for a timeless
value but for some present, incarnate, and imperfect good,
may seem a strange doctrine. But in that way a philosophy
of history is extended into the region of ethics. Ethical
theory has suffered from an inability to settle for limitation
and commitment, while history, and the men who make it,
have been forced to treat every aim as called for by particular situations. Action proceeds from limit, and it arrives at
no finality, but only at another defective result. Yet defect,
in principle, has no critic. There is no platform beyond

limit from which one may snipe at it. Defect secures no systematic condemnation.

Commitment is the acceptance of the relatively static as the locus of values, and the base of action. This may, perhaps, be illustrated by means of what Whitehead called the fallacy of simple location. No location is absolute, but it is just as true that some location must be taken to be absolute in order to make any measurement of relative velocities. This is the factor of limit. Without this limit there is no spatial or temporal infinity. For these, and all other infinities, are only the form of finitude. The same considerations apply in morals or in politics. Every moral judgment rests on the base of a current concern, on what one now identifies oneself as doing. The rules of morals can do no more than maintain that enterprise. The Kantian morality appears defective on this point. There is no duty nor any rationality until the non-rational and existent moment gives leverage to the moral law. The question "What ought I to do?" can get no answer, because it makes no sense, until one is already doing something which has for oneself an uncompromising value. This is the idea of the relatively static. There can be no hope of disinterestedness in the *end* of endeavor, where the actual commitments of men are not already disinterested. The sportiveness of the sequel is only the extrapolation of the disinterestedness of the origin. Only a pure actuality can propose a pure ideality. Commitment and the relatively static are two concepts which emerge from the problem of history. They are articulations of finitude, and they are ontological categories.

In this situation one must, of course, discover the dark depths of the non-rational immediacy. Our acts engage with universality only in one or another of its dimensions. It is this situation which Professor Tillich calls the demonic. When we identify ourselves in any way with the actual it is in some partial aspect of the actual. For example, we may operate on the assumption that the economic order as it occurs in the market place embodies the pattern of our social life and private will. Thereupon the pursuit of commodity threatens to override other interests. It becomes demonic. It may violate other dimensions of our society and of our private wills. It generates ruthlessness and a remarkable opacity to the common humanity of employees. It obscures art, science, religion, or politics. It generates conflict. And yet, this dark partiality of the economic demon is the condition for testing both its own authority and the authority of other interests. For they too may, and I believe must, become demonic. This has happened to religion, to nationalism, and even to education. History rides on the vehicles of partial truth, but their demonry is the sole condition of discovering their force. This is a situation analogous to that in psychology, where the drives or instincts of men can be separated from vagrancy and whim only as they generate conflict and the resultant requirement for a controlled integrity. It is only a philosophy which endows limit with ontological status which can turn conflict to constructive use. The use of conflict is the disclosure of the necessary. To make that disclosure is the labor of history.

These considerations centering on the structure of commitment and leading to the idea of conflict may be carried further in raising afresh the question of universality in history. For history shows men divided among themselves and within themselves. The philosopher has traditionally sought the universal. History in its emphasis on the local and actual seems to disregard the universal. History divides; philosophy unites. History defines relative disorder; philosophy aims to dispel disorder in a coherent picture of all experience.

It is indeed the discontinuity of experience which may first arrest the student and lead him to wonder about its structure. One discovers, for example, that one may not find it easy or possible to comprehend the Greek world, even as it gets presented in its literature, or represented by scholars. We do not offer human sacrifice like Agamemnon, worship nature gods, construct ideal societies without mentioning "rights" as did Plato, or believe in final causes with Aristotle. It is not so much a question of approval or disapproval as of understanding their world, or their outlook. The Greeks are not modern people with recognizable idiosyncracies, but in many respects unrecognizable. Similar considerations apply to all the great formulations of the past. There is a sense of helplessness when the teacher, making a reference say to the *Book of Genesis,* or the *Book of Job,* or the seven deadly sins, or to sin itself, discovers that some students meet these indications with complete blankness. There seems more afoot than an absence of information. Nor can one quickly proceed to inform the ignorant one of the factual content of Plato's *Republic* or the *Book of Job.* One can't just look something up in the *World's Almanac* or the encyclopedia. Facing the past we all have our shortcomings, and they are more grievous than ignorance. They suggest an incompleteness in our selves, in the degree to which one has objectified one's own axioms and habits. The past is historical because it is always relatively discontinuous with the present. Spengler, making it absolutely discontinuous, at least in theory, offers in the end an ahistoric account of past time. Yet, when one first meets the Greek or the medieval mind one may be deeply puzzled, wondering what common humanity unites our day with theirs. History, which vanishes if the discontinuous be made absolute, confronts us with problems of continuity. On the other side, if the past presented no puzzle all transactions in time would appear transparent to a single perspective, and to any perspective.

The humane scholar cannot but experience a sense of shock when the emancipated critic ventures either to approve or condemn the past, its ways and beliefs. Nor is this feeling due to any agreement with those ways. They are gone, and they are not ours. The shock appears because of the implications of such judgments. For they condemn history to the ahistoric. History is more than the sympathetic apprehension of the deeds, thoughts, and feelings of others. It is the activity by which such sympathy can become actual. And that requires effort. This effort is launched by the obscurity of the present itself. Of this need of the present for the clarifying power of the past, the Common Law seems to me as good an illustration as any. What we mean by rights, for example, is discovered in the crises which have led to their assertion. The concepts employed in the law find their meaning in Constitutional history and nowhere else. There is no merely present legal system, none that lacks the continuing pressure of the will which still sustains its functioning. Similar considerations apply to philosophy, where every controlling term means what it has come to mean in the controversies which alone give it authority. An idea must make good, it must make its way. No problem in philosophy is innocent, none is timeless, none is launched from a point of view without environment. That environment is ideal, because it is historical.

We cannot escape history, and we cannot escape the study of history. Nor is there any history at all apart from the thrust of present meanings into their yesterdays. History is a category because it is a necessary condition of the present. In history time is efficacious. This is not so in physics. The efficacy of time occurs only in the strenuous preservation of the present. One is not at liberty to refrain from the study of history. To do so is to court the punishment of which Descartes spoke. Like all proper philosophic punishments it is radical and destructive, for it means that one has sentenced oneself to ostracism from every compulsion, and hence has lost one's freedom. For freedom is the self-control and the self-revision of thought in the modes of necessity.

In summary: history avoids finality, establishes finitude, defines the relatively static, emerges from commitment and conflict, allies us with evil, and presents the universal as self-revision in terms of the necessary. It is the locus of punishment of a systematic sort, and thus becomes an ingredient in any account of the real. It is the most concrete of all categories, and one of the latest to emerge.

The literature of the philosophy of history grows apace, and has captured a remarkable degree of popular interest. This fact should lead to no implication of any lack of technical complexity or philosophic importance. Our times face the broad problems of morale without the traditional comforts of a supernatural support, or for that matter, the support of a rational order of nature which offers us both emancipation from superstition and unlimited means of private satisfaction. We are on our own. In consequence our acts and purposes lack adequate authority. Since they are identifiable only in time, they seem insubstantial and ephemeral. There has resulted a great sense of loneliness so that the return of any public man to the church makes news and seems arresting out of all proportion to the record of mankind in taking it for granted that time is not of the essence. Without a moral universe men become lonely and pessimistic, and sometimes merely trivial. But a moral universe is something more than a cozy refuge from uncertainty. Such an interpretation does less than full justice to the motives that seek it. To be moral is more than being good, or being secure; it is rather being effective. The effectiveness of finitude is the great metaphysical heresy, and, on the whole, the idea of action has fared badly in ultimate formulations.

The idea of a moral universe is not the same as that of a benevolent universe. It is rather the idea of the primary influence of the forces which discover the meaning of good and evil, and therefore include both. This distinction is generated by time, and in time attains progressive refinement. Such a statement is plausible only if time itself may be endowed with the status of an absolute. Where time is invalid, its fruits are tainted. Moral theory apart from history has become, I believe, stale, flat, and unprofitable. We play moral finger exercises with hedonism or with obligation, but make no music so long as action is itself disqualified.

Of the bearing of this idea of a moral universe on the philosophy of history I can give only these shabby indications. But the main lines of the problem have been plotted. The phrase "moral universe" is probably not gladly heard, and, for my part, not gladly used. It seems pretentious. On the other hand it seems absurd to look away from the issues which reintroduce this concept, and to condemn them in advance because of their outcome. Apart from some essay at establishing a bond among men moral theory has little to say, and probably makes no sense. The idea of history proposes that this bond lies in no finality, but in the overcoming of those systematic and structural discontinuities which generate both conflict and reconciliation. There is no morality where nothing finite possesses absolute status. Clearly, such a claim threatens idolatry, but with no less clarity it is also the condition for discovering idolatry. Only what is itself absolute can discover an absolute antagonist. This is the dialectical process of history, and this mode of our being is itself a discovery of time. For this reason it was said earlier that history is radical empiricism, and, I believe, the only form which clothes disorder with unity. Scientific empiricism, when radical, generates nihilism, and leaves even hypotheses and postulates in a perilous position, at most handy, at worst without meaning, in any case without authority.

History, morality, and truth conspire to elevate the particular and the local. For this reason there is no universal history, no synoptic vision of man in all his attitudes. All history, like all measurement in nature, must have its local absolute. Consequently, American history must have for us a peculiar authority. We levy upon others for the illumination of our own meanings, carrying the lines of inquiry as far afield as may be. It is only in terms of our own forces, and of our own responsibilities, that we can make history. The point of view which makes history is also the sole point of view which can study it. Indeed, there is no reason for studying history at all except for the sake of making it. For only in making history can the past secure efficacy. This localism is not barred from universality. On the contrary it defines it in its own self-maintenance. Nor does this seem to me to imply any lack of reverence and respect. One shows no disrespect in inquiring of a man or of a culture how it contributes to such affirmations as one may make and must make in order to preserve one's own point of view, and hence one's capacity for criticism and revision. The past is important because it contributes to our self-comprehension, but it does not do this in general, but only apropos of our present meaning. This, I submit, is not arrogance or provincialism, but rather the sole evidence of our own sense of responsibility. In history the moral bond becomes practical. There alone it becomes imperative, because defined through the dark determination to give here and now illustrations of the law.

There is one essay in Emerson, the one called "Experience," where for a moment the shadows of limit qualify his happy light. For a moment experience appears in a tempered chiaroscuro. "We live amid surfaces," he says, "and the true art of life is to skate well on them. . . . Men live in their fancy, like drunkards whose hands are too soft and tremulous for successful labor. It is a tempest of fancies, and the only ballast I know is a respect to the present hour. Without any shadow of doubt, amidst this vertigo of shows and politics, I settle myself ever the firmer in the creed, that we should not postpone and refer and wish, but do broad justice where we are, by whomsoever we deal with, accepting our actual companions and circumstances, however humble or odious, as the mystic officials to whom the universe has delegated its whole pleasure for us." In this essay the polarity of the individual and universal, the steady Emersonian theme, is viewed from the position of the incomplete individual. It is a remark which may serve to point up the requirements of the attempt to make the secular sacred.

There are, of course, many questions bearing on the idea of history which have not here been mentioned. Something about the meaning of causality, controls, determinism would be in order, and also a great deal on the function of the artifact or symbol as a factor in defining nature as well as man.

In brief summary: A problem is set for the idea of history by the traditional aspirations of philosophy and by the consequences of that ideal whether speculative or empirical, dogmatic or skeptical. History poses a problem about the centrality of action, and draws into the orbit of strict philosophy all the terminology which gives form to finitude.

Above all, it enforces the absoluteness of limit, and makes liaison between the authority of our concepts and the hazardous acts which give them standing room in time. It is, I believe, the locus of the fusion of reality and humanity. Neither God nor nature can make history, for they are infinite. It is the work of our hands and it is the portrait of our minds.

In conclusion, one may consider the association of scholarship and action. There is no science of what to do next. The proper place for advocacy is in politics where practical penalties and rewards attend practical proposals. But the scholar also wishes to be effective. A philosophy of history no more than any other special branch can tell what to do about taxes or the Marshall Plan. But it can validate the medium in which such decisions get made, and it can enforce consideration of the career of those reflectively derived absolutes which in their present relatively static form make it imperative to reach decisions. Whatever views of man and nature asperse the importance of the medium in which decisions get made invalidate both past and present. Such views will leave action subjective, and hence trivial and arbitrary. It is the function of a philosophy of history to bridge the gulf between essence and existence, and it can do this only in so far as essence becomes historical and existence ideal. This seems to me the summary view of what both motivates and controls investigation and the meaning of history.

7

Freedom as a Characteristic of Man in a Democratic Society

I

It may seem plausible, or even obvious, that any view of man which qualifies him to establish a democratic society will endow him with reason and self-control. And yet, the common phrase "human nature" likewise suggests that the defining trait of man is not his autonomy, but rather a set of fixed properties found by observation and experiment. These properties, one supposes, can thereupon be exploited by the social engineers. And so I wish in the first place to examine the status of "nature" and of things which have a "nature" in order to relate the concept of man's "nature" to that of his freedom.

A principal feature of modern man is his control over the immediate environment. The manifestation and proof of that control are found in technology. For us, as men of this time, the real world is the region of controllable objects and predictable events. To that region of experience and knowledge we give the name "nature," and most of our pedagogy assumes this region as the suitable locus of reliable inquiry. We are likely to feel that all knowledge has nature as its content and object. Furthermore, we are committed to a procedure for getting knowledge which directs our attention and our criteria upon this common objective order.

In so far as we discover what we call "facts" we appeal to that region, and what is not found there meets suspicion. Its general properties we take to be described by physics, and, although there appear to be living "organisms" among the dead "mechanisms" of nature, we are intellectually disposed to reduce the living to the dead. The reduction of biology to chemistry or physics seems a proper conquest of knowledge, and so an opportunity for power and control. In general, we suffer intellectual embarrassment in proposing as knowledge any story which employs an organizing vocabulary other than that suitable for the region of objects.

We want knowledge to be only report, in which every element of value has been laid aside. In this way, a study of human nature becomes at best a description of a peculiar sort of objective event.

Of objects, or types of objects, we say that each has a "nature." By this we mean that it is identifiable through the uniformities of its changes and in its consequent entanglement with other changes in a single and infinite order.

If we speak, in this context, of human nature, consistency and analogy suggest that man, too, is an object of knowledge, and consequently controllable, as are all other facts of nature.

Politics, being a control of human nature, rightly seeks an understanding of what is to be controlled. And when politics comes to be called "political science," there is a strong presumption that human nature would best lend itself to management if it were to have a fixed, objective, and reportorial character like salt or marble, or the motion of the heavenly bodies. It is not uncommon to look for such a fixed nature in psychology, as in lists of instincts and in the laws of the learning process. What to attempt in society or politics becomes a corollary of what man in fact is. Just so, in laying up a wall one takes into consideration the proper mixture of sand, gravel, and cement.

For example, the well known solution of Hobbes to the question of government turns on his unflattering view of human nature, the life of man being "solitary, poor, nasty, brutish, and short." Hobbes did see man as possessed in fact, whether one liked it or not, of a measure of reason, whereby man could manage his more anarchistic tendencies to his larger advantage. I mention Hobbes only to furnish an example of a typical procedure, namely one that begins by showing what man in fact is, in order, secondly, to bring him under control.

There is no doubt that this sort of approach to the question of political order has great influence. Control, we rightly assume, depends on knowledge, and so in turn on an objective report of a "nature," in this case human nature. Yet this procedure causes misgiving, since it places human nature in the same class as all other objects, subject to ambiguous manipulations in the interests of ends which it does not, as object, define. So neither does salt determine its use as condiment or preservative, or calcium carbonate as door-step or gravestone. Although devoted to scientific procedures, we hesitate to accept the status of an object. This is the difficulty imposed by assigning to man a "nature" and then subjecting it to control.

This difficulty involves an old ambiguity. For the concept of human nature appears at both ends of a transaction. It appears first as the factual and objective "nature" which is to be managed, and then secondly as the very source of the values which are to exercise direction and control. To preserve the problem it is necessary to make this distinction, while to keep the distinction is to abandon the essay at strictly objective definition of human nature.

There have been many attempts to avoid this dilemma by viewing the values and the controllers of society as themselves nothing more than examples of quite factual or natural instincts of propensities. This is a technique which casts doubt on the validity and authority of all control by man over himself and others. The hero's alleged authority reduces to the facts about human nature, and therefore converts power into impotence, vision into blindness, and control itself into passivity. It is a case of the blind leading the blind.

The frequency of the *argumentum ad hominem* in political controversy discloses the prevalence of this method for the understanding of human nature. We find the free economy represented as a conspiracy to secure profits; the national state as a plot which, by means of fraud, force, and favor, and by use of suitable seductive symbols, lures men away from the scientific truths about themselves. But, on the other side, those who promise to make "every man a king" are in no better case. They themselves are victims of a ruthless lust for power—seductively disguised as benevolence. Whether one be counted as right wing or left wing, there seems always ready at hand an explanation in terms of the nature of man, for example, that rightists are a greedy lot, and the leftists pathologically adrift, frustrated men in a world they never made, who must destroy every vestige of independence in others so that their own personal nonentity can never be discovered. In these ways, good and evil alike become meaningless to the reportorial method. And so the problem of the fitness of human nature for democracy, or for any other final end, becomes absurd.

It was Francis Bacon who proposed that "knowledge is power." He, likewise, took knowledge to be confined to nature, and he died, it is said, from a cold contracted in an experiment to test the preservative effect of refrigeration on meat. Since Bacon's death in 1636 we have come a long way in knowledge and in the type of control which it yields. Today, our knowledge of nature threatens to destroy us all, and our knowledge of man reduces control to an illusion and a menace. How far this mistrust of knowledge has moved can be gauged from the frequent and derogatory use of the phrase "power politics."

To mistrust power is to mistrust knowledge. Except as willess contemplation knowledge can result only in action, i.e., at an attempt at control. It is this dilemma which underlies Arthur Koestler's book *The Yogi and the Commissar.* One can do anything one likes with knowedge of objects except one thing: one cannot by its means define the free man or the democratic society. So it comes to this, that man fears destruction from his physics and an emasculated will from psychology. Nor should we flatter ourselves that the sharp-eyed explorers of illusion can offer a remedy. For their truth is that of natural knowledge, and they can only stare at the facts where no trace of value can either define aspiration or guide fulfillment.

In summary: "Nature to be commanded must be obeyed." The obedience, however, is for the sake of the command. Knowledge seeks power; and conformity, control. It is command, power, and control which are difficult to define in the context of report.

II

The average citizen exhibits complacency rather than distress over the democratic process. It is those with a theoretical bent who sometimes express misgivings and even despair over the meaning of such words as "freedom" and "self-direction." For these words do not find definition in the context of scientific report. They suggest wilfulness and egoism, and allege a type of control neither statistical nor causal. How is nature, particularly human nature, to be commanded?

The problem of power in a democracy involves the control of men over each other. Yet, one may distrust all such power. It has often been remarked that power corrupts. Consequently, it may be proposed that men be stripped of all power over each other. It is, of course, true that power corrupts. Nothing else can. Impotence can do no harm, nor, of course, any good. Politics is a science of the power of men over themselves and over others. Its meaning vanishes when human nature lacks self-assertion and the passionate egoism which is the spring of all control.

There occurs in this most individualistic age a deep mistrust of power, as, for example, in the national state, even though it be democratic. It is felt in various quarters that the state must wither away, leaving either a bland anarchy, or a parliament of man, where nothing is intolerable except having a will of one's own. Such proposals reflect the suspicion we feel of the power of man over himself and over others.

In so far as man is described as having a "nature," these suspicions seem to me entirely proper. There is no account of man as a fact, or as a part of the region of objects, which can exhibit him as possessed of both power and responsibility. Natural forces are not responsible forces. The naturalistic account of man can only view every pretense of power as an illusion and as a menace. Political science on those premises can set for itself only one task: that of stripping man of this irresponsible illusion. This is a purpose in which, by a curious irony, both naturalists and supernaturalists are in agreement.

Whatever view of man deprives him of power over himself and others solves the political problem by abolishing it. When men are viewed as objects, command becomes simply a mistaken idea, for it violates the condition on which human nature is presumably discovered, namely, as fact and uniformity. Man becomes lost in his "nature," and so far from being in a position to rule others, he cannot even rule himself.

III

On what conditions, then, can one tell a story of man as the locus of responsible power? In terms of the preceding analysis one way of answering this question is barred. It is the way which would look for political and democratic qualifications in objective peculiarities.

A clue to those activities which incorporate both power and responsibility may be found in the identification of the occurrence of tyranny.

One locus of tyranny is revealed in obstacles to the investigation of nature. Science is power not only as a means for technology, but as a primary exhibition of responsible thought. Wherever men by doctrine or by law forbid or hamper the investigation of nature, we detect the mark of oppression and degradation. For science is much more than an enlargement of animal learning. It is also the primary and the most solid region of community. It is not a community of custom, ritual, or habit, or an anthropological pattern of behavior. It is a community of minds in which men exercise power over each other through their vulnerability to criticism. And it is through this freely assumed liability to error that respect is established and men become ends in themselves. No threats, not even those of death and hell-fire, have stayed the mind of man from these adventures. Nor can any promise of bread and circuses summon the energies for the disciplined and ascetic clarification of our common world.

Nature is sometimes debased into a static fact. Any such premise is fatal for the political guidance of free men. Nature is, on the contrary, a historic achievement, always changing in its outlines, and even in its logic. The political scientist who bases his view of man on what he takes to be scientific truth is making a grave error. For all views of nature are achievements, and the mechanical view, itself only three centuries old, and now assailed by positivism, is itself a product of reason. One does not find human nature as an episode within the latest account of physics, but rather, I believe, in those energies and values to which physics owes its genesis and its historical transformations.

I would ask you to consider how a person feels his own reality. Is it otherwise than in effectiveness, i.e., in the exercise of power? Impotence and freedom are mutually exclusive. A premise of the democratic man is his individual reality in the exercise of influence upon others. This, I submit, is the goal of politics for free men: *to create those conditions in which men can influence others in so far as those others are in charge of themselves.* This need is at the bottom of our liberties, of our rights, and of our non-arbitrary powers.

Above all, what characterizes the free man is his capacity

and determination to make history. It is not the static truth that makes men free. In that static guise the truth always enslaves. It is rather in the *revision* of truth that freedom is found. Furthermore, static truth abolishes community. The revision of truth is the maintenance of community, not, of course, the anthropological, or sociological, community, but the community of free men. One cannot argue or deal with static modes of truth. In history, we see the awful, but responsible, spectacle of man's reinterpretations of himself and of nature, and reassessment of our heritage. One can inherit neither truth nor freedom. Every heritage must be understood in its own creative motives and then overpassed in amendment and revision. We cannot escape nature, but neither can we escape history.

These general properties of the democratic man entail many corollaries. As a first consequence may be mentioned the maintenance of systematic thought or inquiry, since only order can be revised, and only the pretention to responsible order can create both humility and accessibility.

A second corollary is this: there must be preserved non-political sources of power, as the centers of privacy and as the authority for the criticism of political institutions. Government is the form of community, but not its substance. It is the sign of the absoluteness of a self-regulating privacy. Politics waxes exuberant and possessive. Modes of non-political self-assertion occur in science, social groups such as the family and private clubs, and in religion and commerce. Man is indeed a social animal, but it would, I believe, be a mistake to interpret his primary sociability as political. When that mistake gets made, there is nothing for it but to treat man as an object, and then he is devoured by the managers who, one hears, know best how to establish community. The state is rather the organization, and the express recognition, of the non-political modes of personal actuality and influence. From this condition flows the authority and the mission of the free state. To extend this recognition is the history-making task of free governments.

A third corollary can be offered: democratic man seeks responsible power without asserting a fixed goal. This is the quality of risk. Security of any sort, made absolute, is the stifling of freedom. A risky, but creative adventure is the man himself. When, by means of action, including experiment, we define our world, we see only oblivion in security. Cosmic security is an anachronism. Personal security is the denial of adventure, the obliteration of personality.

In summary, human nature has no static, objective, or merely cognitive definition. Knowledge is power, but the sort of knowledge sought in politics concerns those traits which allow one, in so far as one is in charge of oneself, to influence others in so far as they, too, are in charge of themselves. Science and history-making are among the major actualities of such power. In consequence, three corollaries were mentioned: the need of systematic thought, of non-political loci of self-government, and finally of risk or adventure. I may conclude with a sentence of Ortega y Gasset: "Man has no nature; he has only a history."

8

The Midworld

I

What I propose is that we consider the price to be paid for enfranchising discourse. Discourse needs authority. It is this concern that lies at the core of the philosophy of history. History deals in what has been done in one way or another. Its materials are the residue of deeds. They are artifacts of every description. The region of artifacts may be called the "midworld" since it is exclusively neither the self nor the not-self, neither consciousness nor its object. This inquiry concerns the status of language, of signs and symbols in their widest sense. It lies between epistemology and metaphysics and is the bridge between them.*

History does not study "nature" conceived as object, or as the region of objects. Nor does it deal with the supernatural in its recondite perfection, although the alleged signs of the supernatural do concern the historian. Nor does it study the stream of consciousness, i.e., psychology. For all these reasons it separates itself from the usual patterns of truth, which are stories about quite impersonal reality. No statement in history concerns the timeless and invariant. As for those sciences which deal with ahistoric modes of order, history regards them as the record of experience, not

---

*If this essay were to be rewritten today, the term *functioning object* would generally be used where the term *artifact* now appears. The next essay offers a brief discussion of the distinction between the terms.

as true, but as the expression of what we have regarded to be true.

It is concerned, therefore, with finitude and its career. But in this respect, history seems to alienate itself from the traditional concerns of philosophy, which have tended to stress the timeless and the ahistoric, treating time as a derivative and secondary. The true heavenly city, we have supposed, is not built by hands, and the true forces of nature sweep man and his deeds into the invariance of their own law. We have been trying to see all things under the aspect of eternity. It cannot be denied that such conditions of rising superior to time have their attractions. Yet many have felt that they must settle for something closer, finding a sharper and more self-possessed life within limitation.

Limitation has not been accorded an equal place at the high table of philosophy. It sits well below the salt unless, indeed, it has been only a servant in the festivities of its betters. This is what the historian knows and so, metaphysically homeless, he has maintained a stubborn or even sardonic independence, occupied with the identification of individual moments. It would appear, and I would propose, that unless history be a "category," there can be no philosophy of history. But if it be such, then the region of its concern, artifacts, or the midworld, must be accorded a place among the constitutional elements of being.

This need of providing for artifacts is the specter that haunts philosophers and their discourse. And it seems plain that one could not exorcise that perturbed spirit by further incantations.

II

In this way, arrested by the insecure status of our own words, we encounter a variant of skeptical mistrust. In philosophy we must use language. We speak our minds. We speak them, too, in practices and institutions, themselves artifacts, church, state, art, science, and language itself.

They confront us as the loci of both order and confusion. In discourse we no longer deal with abstract appearance and abstract reality, but with a midworld which is also our own deed. And so, being our own, it is threatened with a lack of ontological status.

Skepticism traditionally occurs as self-mistrust. We are not skeptics, however, because we make mistakes, but because we can no longer trust the means of deciding. Nobody is less skeptical than the canny person who knows wooden nickels when he sees them. Skepticism is no grubby caution. It is a point of arrest where we are thrown back on our own resources. And those we have no reason to trust. On the other side, neither can we trust anything else. It is in this situation that the properly emotional and distracted mood of skepticism appears. We cannot bridge what Professor J. B. Pratt called "the epistemological gulf" since we are incapable of moving either way between appearance and reality. It is this situation which some have thought to identify as the province of epistemology.

In this way skeptical insecurity marks the experience of elementary self-assertion, the disclosure that we are parties to our affirmations and denials, although, of course, we hardly see how that leaves us with a satisfactory result. But this is also the threshold of responsibility, a stage of all thought as it passes from confident innocence to the dark menace of egoism. Skepticism shows, too, that thoughtfulness as a power in the world is first identified in the threat to its own trustworthiness. Confidence in thought and its works cannot be original. It must be twice-born.

But while no original position, neither can skepticism be final. So we have to look for ways out of it. These ways have not, characteristically, given finitude an ontological status. In realism and mysticism discourse lacks constitutional authority. Both confront thought in the end with some overpowering and absorbing reality. In realism the disparity between appearance and reality is allegedly maintained, but not bridged. In mysticism, the disparity is abolished.

A solution should not only unite the factors. It should also *keep them apart* as the price of the problem. Until separated they cannot be reconciled. It has sometimes seemed that the division represented a miscarriage of thought, that it ought not to have occurred and that it exhibits nothing more than the folly of metaphysics.

Of the confusion there can be no doubt. But its necessity is no less obvious if thought is to be discovered as an efficacy, and its works accredited. The primary efficacy of thought is to discover itself, something that could not occur in bland security or in complete rational fluency.

But, then, this situation is as long as it is broad. For neither could the *object* be discovered in principle until it became systematically elusive. That the self is elusive many have been pleased to note, and, indeed, its fortunes as an entity, or as a content of consciousness, have been pretty dismal. But the object is no less obscure. Nothing is object by virtue of any specific attribute. Object like subject is an omnibus word. If it is to be useful it must be identified through a formal order, as constitution, not as datum or even hypothesis.

It is the *necessity* of the distinction between object and subject which was neglected by traditional skepticism and, as it turned out, by the psychological empiricism which was its offspring. The ground of the distinction could not be some matter of fact, some clear or naively apprehended object. The troubled experience of skepticism is not to be understood in calm passivity. It falls within no placid environment of any sort, natural, psychological, or logical.

In this way it is the deepest frustration and the first compulsion. It is the birth of responsibility because it forces us away from abstractions into a more concrete account of its occasion. It does this because it can give no account of itself, *in terms of the absolute disparities which generate its impasse.* It is a conflict without ground in the articulate. It can become articulate only as it is reinterpreted through limited and actual modes of imperfect order.

A classic illustration of this blockade of abstractions occurs in the *Theaetetus.* I will quote a few lines to show that the above dialectics are not without provocation.

The problem of the *Theaetetus* is that of establishing knowledge, but it is presented as an inquiry into the possibility of error. Plato, it seems to me, is clear on the locus of the difficulty, namely the exclusiveness of the distinction between knowledge and ignorance. He asks:

"Where, then, is false opinion? For if all things are either known or unknown there can be no opinion which is not comprehended under this alternative, and false opinion is excluded." At the end of the dialogue he observes: "But how utterly foolish when we are asking what is knowledge, that the reply should be, 'right opinion with knowledge of difference' or of anything!" This, he says, is to "go round and round" and to be "as the blind directing the blind."

III

We need an articulate basis for skepticism and it will furnish, I hope, a first hold on the midworld. What seems called for is something more concrete to work with than appearance and reality, or knowledge and ignorance. The defect of such terms is that they furnish us with no ordered materials, mere appearance which is states of mind, and mere reality which nobody knows anything about, or, if he does, he can't say what it is without adulteration. It is not the case that Plato's difficulty resulted from the conflict of relatively ordered areas of experience; it resulted from a total *lack of order* and of actuality, in both of them. Conflict needs an articulate vehicle.

That is the price of conflict. Each factor must exercise some hold upon us as an already established area of reason and control. At the same time, neither can be adequate to the whole scope of our practice and belief. Reason never occurs in any actual integrity, but is pluralistic and partial. That is why we are involved with it, and why we know about it. We don't have, and we can't have, an infinite organism. We find ourselves, for example, somewhat involved in the practices and beliefs which turn on value control, i.e., where events find their explanation in ends. So we have a rationale in ethics, politics, aesthetics, in the maintenance of individuality and free government. On the other side, it would be difficult to disavow our profound commitment to impersonal types of change where, as in physics, value control is excluded. In consequence, we stand divided in our needs and loyalties, in our practices and beliefs.

In this situation, each component of conflict carries some claim to order within itself. There is the control of value, and of causality. There is the integrity of the individual on his own, and there is the vast impersonality of nature's laws. Here is plenty of difficulty, but however reduced to abstract terms it draws its vitality from actual and concrete organizations of experience.

It follows from this that the occasion of an articulate skepticism is retrospective, as indeed are all reflective moments. Something reasonable and self-defining, as well as nature-defining is already established. Our unease reflects also our previous grasp. This is the embarrassment of skepticism, its self-consciousness and awkwardness, its misery and also its progress from the naive. But this self-consciousness is not analogous to the presence of an error. Where we find ourselves in error we presume we have command of the order which has been violated. But here in skeptical self-consciousness, the threat of confusion becomes systematic, because it is the confusion of what we most trust, modes of reason themselves.

It may be useful to remind ourselves briefly that this concrete skepticism depends on no specific conflict. For one it marks the impasse of empiricism and rationalism; for another home influence and college-learned doctrines. But in all cases it appears as the conflict of commitments each of which is articulate, although a vehicle of but a partial reason. Thus, the *occasion* of skepticism, *not just its solution,* as Descartes proposed, is existential. It is not theoretical merely. It is not merely tentative, passive, and receptive. It is not positivistic but the consequence of universality in the actual. It is not the consequence of a vaulting ambition that o'erleaps itself, but of something far more modest and far more turbulent.

I hope it is plain that I set some store by the necessity of skepticism. Of course, I do not mean by this necessity that skepticism falls within an environment which produces it. It is rather *the loss of confidence in whatever one regards as environment.* Nor, of course, would I suppose that there is any intellectual technique for producing it. One can't be argued into it. All that is question-begging. Skepticism is rather the point at which necessity occurs as an idea, for there one is threatened with the nullification of such actual control as everyone in a degree possesses. But it has great heuristic value in bringing to notice the condition of its occurrence.

Finally, one would not want to say that skepticism occurs as a conflict among or between abstract absolutes. Yet, in itself it is the actuality, and so the absoluteness, of conflict. That is a distinction worth making. There are philosophies averse to all assurance, and others which would not care to find their origin in conflict, with all that is thereupon implied. Not all will see necessity in the conditions for maintaining the order of finitude.

In broad summary, skepticism is difficult to define because it is throughout reflective. It occurs as conflict. This conflict is not between abstract appearance and abstract reality, but between already ordered modes of experience. In these we have a stake, and to them we are committed precisely because they are the vehicles of as much grasp and comprehension as we already possess. Skepticism is retrospective, and it is existential. It occurs through no specific opposition, but through any systematic opposition. Consequently it is the occasion for discovering what one does actually consider orderly and systematic. At the same time, by demanding a decision as to the true order, or as to the relations among modes of order, it forces upon us responsibility for our world. After skepticism, our commitments are deliberate and cannot be disavowed as not our own.

IV

Assurance must assert its force in the very materials which permit articulate doubt. Otherwise it will again take wing into some noumenal or transcendent region and so relegate finitude and its actual expression to further metaphysical ostracism. Of that there has, it seems to me, been quite enough. In a time of decision, philosophy can hardly allow itself to become an adventure into enervation. Nor, in a time when arbitrariness has taken new and dangerous forms can philosophy avoid seeking a humanistic solution to problems of authority. Like other responsible studies it must, I believe, express limitation, but in its particular case limitation must stand its ground as the actual locus of responsibility. It seems to me that nothing else could be proposed by men who wish to be both resolved and critical.

There can be no question that nature and society do, in structure and content, enlist our thought and will. How, then, do they come to possess such authority? This is the crux of the problem, and it leads directly to the artifact, and the articulate regions which depend on the artifact for their order, and are allied to it in content. The thesis takes some such form as this: *There is no fact without an artifact.* Language, or expression in its widest sense, is the *locus of the union* of the abstractly subjective and the abstractly objective. It is here suggested that apropos of this union limitation acquires ontological status. There the subject is embodied, and the object becomes the vehicle of meaning, and in some cases of quite formal and ideal meanings. There are different sorts of artifacts, notably signs and symbols, but for the moment I will leave those distinctions in abeyance and deal with the situation more generally.

Perhaps an illustration would serve to carry the reflection which voices the theme. Space, a property of articulate nature, occurs in measurement. It is the order of simultaneous diversity. Things are at a distance and a determinate distance. But while such ideas as "distance" and "measurement" seem common enough, they have given a good deal of trouble. One reason is that they have no psychological equivalents. There is no sense organ for the apprehension of space. It is no specific quality, no datum of a discrete and peculiar sort. It is not here or there, now or then. It is no accident, falling within some already defined situation identifiable and organized without benefit of space. Nor is it something remembered, or something imaginatively constructed from materials devoid of it. Then there is the view that space is a universal and *a priori* form, pervading all experience, distinctive of none.

For some reason, and I am convinced that there is a reason, "space" has rated more tolerance than other universals or *a priori* forms, such as substance, causality, or mind. One might wonder how one is to play favorites among them. At any rate, while the critique of cause has proceeded with a good deal of vigor, space has enjoyed a relative respectability. This immunity has been especially notable in view of the highly rated rule that no concept which fails to make a local and specific difference can win full faith and credit as a factor of the actual world. Of course, no constitutional universal could meet that demand if what one requires is a distinctive appearance.

Space, however, does have a finite actuality as well as a universal ideality. In the case of space this limited actuality is the yardstick. At first sight this may seem absurdly simple and inadequate. The yardstick is an actual object, a *functioning object*. One can, and indeed one must, take it in hand. It is palpable. It is a piece of pine or maple, and so part of the whole collection of objects. It may, or course, be made of any other material, a textile strip or a steel tape. It is not by virtue of one material or another that the identification "yardstick" is made. Nor does it possess any peculiar sense qualities. Good workmen, and men of science, shrink from using it as a tool, as a device for propping a window or poking the fire. That is not to use it, but to abuse it. Yet such abuse is surely not any consequence of its material composition. It does very well to prop a window. Nor, though not to be used as a tool by any decent man, is it a fetish, something not to be handled, or handled only with sentimentality, or with awe, or for the invocation of occult powers. If it is no tool, it serves no purpose and is quite destroyed when treated as an aid in getting adjusted to the alleged environment.

Nor is a yardstick a yard long. A piece of cloth may be a

yard wide, or a target 500 yards away, because one has determined their spatial extent through application of the
yardstick as a unit of measure. Nor, of course, must that
unit be a yard. Horses are said to be so many "hands"
high. "Full fathom five thy father lies." "Give him an inch
and he'll take an ell."

There are other peculiarities of yardsticks and I submit
that as one considers this apparently absurd simplicity it
may be said to take on dimensions, and indeed, to become a
first-class puzzle. One may note that the yardstick cannot
be produced by what is called "ostensive definition." It is
no illustration of a prior subjectivity in a prior objectivity
where there already exists a here and there and every sort of
spatial order. It conforms to no idea in the mind where, by
hypothesis, the mind is furnished with plenty of other
ideas unaffected by spatial order. It is not a possible idea like
the Loch Ness monster whose appearance coincides with
the tourist season, nor is it like the celebrated sea-serpent
with red wings. It is no possibility belonging to the null
class, nor yet in a class with members. And neither does it
exist in the pure infinity of universal space.

Nor is it a convention. That is a question-begging term
in this context. A particular unit may be a convention, but
not the unit in principle. Conventions do not define the situation into which they are introduced; red and green lights
do not define roads and vehicles or account for them.

With this budget of characterization before us, some reflection on the numerous peculiarities of the yardstick
seems in order. Of central importance is the union in this
familiar instrument or symbol of both subjective and objective factors. Here is all the psychology that anyone could
ask for in the apprehension of an object. Here, similarly, is
all the neutrality to psychology which appears among the
common objects of nature. But the yardstick conveys a further property, that of its *ideality,* and that is the feature
which I wish to underscore, and, if possible, make clear.
This ideality turns on the function or role of the yardstick.
Through it, nature, in respect of its simultaneous diversity,
gets established. Nature as space occurs as the actual opera-

tion of measurement. In its infinity, it indicates the endless extension of an actual and finite object in its use and function. One cannot ask of a unit of measure whether it has application. It is such a unit precisely in that application and for no other reason. Spatial infinity is the order of finitude. But finitude has no order at all unless some *object,* something here and now, is invested with an ideal meaning. Nor has infinity any order until the artifact or symbol becomes its vehicle and present reality.

The region of which the yardstick is a part is itself dependent on measurement for its order. For that reason the region of objects exerts a stubborn tenacity, and resists attempts to reduce it to psychology, or even to phenomenal status. This stubbornness of the objects of nature and of the perceptions associated with nature derives its force from the union of subject and object embodied in the artifact and its implications. Otherwise we might easily let nature go.

On the other side, the transcendent *fails* to exert this spontaneous hold upon us. In its traditional forms it is not defined through us, nor is it sustained through the order of symbols, as are all modes of articulate and ideal infinity. Consequently, the perpetuation of any infinite being as an object of regard, involving as it does the disqualification of limit, becomes a tour de force. Education then operates as training and indoctrination, and belief is enforced by reward, punishment, and abnegation. Here, indeed, we will find ritual and symbolism, but the symbols will not be those objects through which nature secures articulation and the mind its exercise. This is a theme capable of some extension as one respectfully considers those vast endeavors to express and summon the energies of men in terms of the symbolism of the transcendent. The yardstick, the monument, the word, in contrast, are the *functioning symbolism of finitude* and propose both the infinity of nature and of the resources of soul.

But, while functioning objects illuminate no hypostatized infinity, neither do they assist in giving order to that version of finitude which leaves it nominalistic. These two—an infinity which is a *fait accompli,* and a finitude without universality—are *alike* in their repudiation of actuality which is also ideal. Neither is articulate because neither accords organizing power to, or has any ontological place for, yardsticks. Each, in its own way, can do nothing with discourse but leaves it arbitrary, and therefore non-rational. It is the functioning object that unites the particular and the universal. They are united in function, or in use, in the embodiment of form. The embodiment of form is function.

The reality of a world is a consequence of the reality of its functioning parts. Where nothing finite is real, and I mean metaphysically beyond question, neither is anything infinite comprehensible. That is beyond question which permits questions to be asked, and any question is the mark of limitation, yet of reason and articulation too. In stressing the priority of the whole, philosophy has been driven to devices to account for the parts. Their generation was a mystery. Their order at best phenomenal. On the other side, parts without order are in no better case. A *determinate infinity* rests upon the actuality of its ideal symbol.

Not to apprehend objects as the reality of formal order is to view them subjectively. For the intellect they become mere appearance, and for the will mere desire or aversion. This is what Ortega fears in *The Revolt of the Masses,* the reduction of the complex world of the past to appearance and appetite. He fears the assault upon reason and upon persons, those who have spoken in the significant forms which make up the actual and intelligible world. It has seemed useful to cast a passing glance at this negative side of the picture, in order to make plainer our involvement with the midworld and the stake we have in it. For it must be admitted that so fragile and even common-place an object as the yardstick hardly promises, when first regarded, to illustrate a point of some importance, as I see it, in the establishment of a metaphysical foundation for history and all other modes of man's deeds.

Order, once said to be heaven's first law, and then alleged to reside in an objective nature, or in a phenomenal vision, we must now, I propose, relocate in the midworld. As a matter of fact this, and nothing else, is the material of all studies. Physics, for example, studies no order except that of its instruments. The order of physical nature is the theory of their use. History is wholly confined to things done, although theories about history sometimes attempt to force it into dependency on psychology, physics, or theology. It may be noted too, that the persuasion of realities disjoined from man and his deeds has grown apace with the enlargement of his own articulate powers. Heaven seems never so sure as when the pealing organ blows, or when the arguments of a Thomas or an Edwards exert their compulsions. Nature, similarly, seems now well established, so that it seems folly to propose a midworld as its condition. But this is a systematic illusion and it is surprising to see how rapidly it collapses once we suppose that, as a matter of course, our most solid realities would, of necessity, be precisely those whose infinity echoed the order inherent in the finite symbol. The midworld, I believe, robs nobody of nature. On the contrary, it is the means of saving nature from an arbitrary dominance, and of then preventing its inevitable dissolution in the acids of skepticism.

Here too, I venture to suggest, empiricism can take authority, no longer groping for an order which its own requirements have forced it to disqualify, but without which its critical pretensions are absurd. To save us from the unverifiable it has bombarded all our citadels, with the result usual in bombardments, reduction to rubble. The assumption of criticism is that we shall have a world of our own, and should that *not* be the outcome it won't matter much what that alien world will be. But what we must have is then to be not only our own, but also a *world;* and so empiricism has exhausted itself in trying to have it both ways on premises which make it impossible to have it either way.

The broad demands of a philosophy of history require the authentication of discourse and a construction placed upon *functioning objects*. But discourse is language and it is a deed. Accordingly it is limitation. The knowledge of limit as a systematic factor—and it can appear in no other way—occurs in skepticism. Traditional skepticism posed the problem of uniting appearance and reality, but the complementary problem of holding them apart is no longer pressing. In fact, actual skepticism always involves relatively rational and concrete conflict. When that is unrecognized solutions take the form of reductionism or phenomenalism. The ground of the distinction between the skeptical absolutes is the artifact, or the symbol, because it is the local and actual embodiment of ideality and of criticism. It generates infinities, but only as the form of an actual finitude and an ideal finitude. It is the reason for the stake we have in nature and institutions. In its extension it is the midworld, the basis of a responsible humanism.

V

By way of further illustration of the midworld something should be said about words and language. Here, again, the problem is to discover the part played by words in making possible the order of subjects and objects.

It was once supposed that words possessed magical properties, and very likely something of the sort is true. They were supposed to exert forces, or to be capable of summoning them. "I can call spirits from the vasty deep," said Glendower. One gives one's word, no small thing to do. Robert Frost, in "The Code" shows how New Englanders of rural habit watch their words. Jacob sought his father's blessing, and was willing to play a trick to get it.

In any case one can hardly be casual about words. They are mysterious enough. As they occur they seem quite ordinary sounds, like wind and wave, or, when written, sights, like sticks and stones. Their perception enlists no strange or unusual faculties. Shall we then say that words fall into the same order of appearance as other objects?

There are difficulties. The objects of nature rest in their own invariance. They are what they appear to be and nothing more. Nature, so regarded, tells no tales, proposes no points of view. It is infinite in its integral impersonality. So, it has no language and makes no sign. This aloofness has often enough been noted. In nature as object there are no confusions, mistakes, truths, virtues, or conflicts. It exhibits no historical changes. Language and artifact are what nature, as object, cannot produce. Naturalism finds no *subject* among the objects. But it seems more serious not to find an artifact. For, while the sufficiency and order of nature might be menaced by the *presence* of spirit, they are even more menaced by the *absence* of a symbol.

Language seems an intruder among proper objects which, in their well-mannered regularity, exhibit no feeling, and make no errors. Their ways are not modified by signs, and so are not established by them. How language managed to enter that region has seemed to call for a theory. Such a theory should not, however, invoke for language any environment which is itself identified through artifacts. That would be begging the question. What is more, it would fail to account for exactly that aspect of an artifact which makes it a sign, rather than another object or quality of an object. This situation seems to me a recurrent one in philosophy. All the embodiments of finitude, a work of art, the constitution of a state, the processes of history, seem incidental to the quite impersonal region in which they are episodes. All seem to need a theory to explain them, and all need the same sort of theory, one namely on terms quite other than their own. The inarticulate, however, can hardly be proposed as the control of the articulate.

In passing, it might be amusing to consider why we might not set out to abolish language. For, if language were really an *incident* of experience we might hope to control its occurrence, as we take antitoxin for typhoid before going on a journey. It seems hard, just because one is dealing with language, to deny that what has a causal genesis in an environment cannot be controlled in its causes. Knowledge is power. Nature to be commanded need only be obeyed. But I do not think we will be able to put a stop to it. At bottom, the reason is that to do so would be to abolish nature as an identifiable region and also in detail.

Discrimination among objects depends on identifying them through names, a point made with uncommon clarity, I think, in Suzanne K. Langer's *Philosophy in a New Key*. Perception is never direct. It is something more than a combination of sense data plus the psychological functions of memory and imagination. An object with a name is consolidated. It possesses a unity lacking in passive perception. It acquires that unity through the factor of action. Names are our deeds. Objects acquire names as part of our control over them. No appearance has any significance when it lacks association with the act which establishes its place in the economy of mind. One sees little in a walk through the woods if the names of trees, plants, birds, or conformations of terrain are unknown. The long analysis of perception into passive ingredients, purged of dreaded distortions of the subject, led to the denial of necessary connections and to the insignificance of appearances. Action places the object in a continuum of other objects and endows them with its own order.

Action is never direct. An object isolated from a situation in which no prior marks of action can be found calls for no specific response. One does not know what to do about it. Suppose one is lost in the woods and one is thirsty. A slope suggests a brook at the bottom. The slope becomes a sign of water. But this is not because there are sensible qualities about a slope, rather than about a peak, to offer the suggestion. It lies there like any other object. As object alone it gives no sign. But if one has ever walked down a slope to water, if the slope is mixed with action, it takes on an added quality of significance. The general rule is this: A sign occurs only through prior action.

A sign is both the occasion of an act and the evidence of a prior act. Our acts, in turn, are known to us in proportion to our identification of objects. The slope is a sign. It is also an object. And it is also an appearance. *The sign is an appearance which controls the production of other appearances.* Nature is controlled appearance. This is the foundation of our trust in experiment. Even observation is not an unguided receptivity. It is a controlled receptivity through signs and through functioning objects like microscopes, or a compass.

The control of appearance is the same as the objective.

That is the only ground for the revelation of objects in principle. *Objects are those appearances which I can produce by action guided by other objects which, already touched by action, serve as signs.* In passivity there are no objects or any subjects either. That is the well known and quite proper result of that empiricism which is based on analysis alone.

Language does not supervene upon nature or upon the self. It is the evidence of control, and only in terms of control can either of the two abstract components be identified. Without it both are lost, along with every vestige of order. It is not unusual to treat language as formal within itself; what seems less usual is to assert that language is in principle a formality, a type of order dialectically related to the order of nature and self and necessary for both.

Language is not a uniform and unambiguous symbolism such as one finds in mathematics and symbolic logic. Signs as language are always the marks of broken worlds. There is not one language, but many, and each person and society has to some extent his own. This is one of the true bases of pluralism, of the actuality of finitude. Communication is not the mark of complete agreement, but of partial agreement. To seek for monism in language is to betray oneself as occupying the ahistoric bias of traditional philosophy.

Communication implies a limited world and a vulnerable one. To seek the invulnerable in nature, in the supernatural, or in some coercive symbolism is to destroy all signs, and all functioning objects. There is no communication through objects viewed as wholly impersonal, or yet through subjects viewed as wholly personal. The role of communication is disclosed in its collapse. The disclosure of its function and properties occurs in those conflicts which threaten it in principle. Those conflicts, on the side of the psychological, lead to madness, with all its inaccessibility. On the side of relatively controlled reality they appear as the disparities of outlooks. It is at that point, and not short of it, that we feel the menace of privacy. Then, for the first time, the relation of speech to nature and to other men looms with existential force. That is why I regard philosophy as the deliberate concern with the loci of systematic conflict. It is the function of language to permit such conflicts to occur, and thereby enforce the acknowledgment of its role in history.

For history is the revision of outlooks at the point of conflict between them. It is the process of putting us in rapport with each other, and with those monuments of expression which are the substance of civilization.

So, at the end, we move, it seems to me, once more into finitude which, because of language in its widest sense, operates as the maintainer of the distinction between self and nature and between selves. This is the locus of all criticism, of all disorder and so of all control. It is a concrete situation, but at the same time defined throughout in form and ideality.

I may say in conclusion that I have found this general position fruitful. How are philosophers to look with tolerance and even with envy on each other's specialties? How is one to bring discourse about history, the state, aesthetics, or logic under a common roof? What I missed in the realisms current in my student days and for some time thereafter was an ability to open pathways to those varied areas. Each appeared as a novelty and some as illicit. But it seems to me that in terms of a view based on the ontological status of finitude all the forms of discourse which exhibit limited but actual essays in orderly language can find a home. On the other side, the majestic idealisms, learned and humane, sympathetic and hospitable, seemed to ignore precisely these dark emergencies which are the occasion of desperate attempts to maintain civic order and personal integrity. For these very good general reasons, as well as for the more specific reasons of this essay it seems to me that one could do worse than consider the ontological status of the midworld. In its disciplined energies, ideal and finite, all expression can be interpreted. Otherwise we shall go on doing violence to our deeds as we force them into alien contexts, or else leave them in the limbo of phenomena.

9

Functioning Objects, Facts, and Artifacts

Arrowheads rate as artifacts; they are not found in nature. They are tools, instrumental aids. They serve a purpose. Any tool serves a special need, facilitates a desired result. For certain purposes a crosscut saw serves less well than a ripsaw, a screwdriver than a hammer. "Artifact" is a term more restrictive than "tool." A stone may be a tool but is not an artifact designed for a purpose, not exhibiting design, art, craft, or skill. The anthropologist does not come upon man until he discovers the artifact, a revelation of *local control,* that is, something done at a specific place and time. Man is an artisan; he makes artifacts. Find an artifact and you encounter a man; find a stone and you do not. The artifact is an awesome revelation. At hazard—it is an incorporate psyche. An absurd contradiction? Better not to say so if one speaks of artifacts.

Facts and artifacts differ. We are supposed to have had no hand in the facts. The iron law of knowledge commands that we Keep Out. But someone has not kept out of revelatory artifacts. They betray a purpose; the facts do not. The artifact is an actuality, the fact a passivity. The fact is impersonal; the artifact individuates the maker, his tribe, his intelligence, his "culture." The artifact leads to history and to dated time; the fact invokes an undated order as the price of not being rejected as an illusion. The artifact reveals an agent and the tribal range of skill; the fact derives its status and authority from its immunity to interference or control by any individual at a place or time. The fact is anonymous. No purpose can improve the facts, but it can improve the efficiency of a stone arrowhead or of a steam engine. The incorporate mind is the only mind ever discovered. It eludes the passive psychology of "data." To speak at great hazard: The only word is the incarnate word.

Nature has always been characterized in the terms of action. Animistic nature reflected the abruptness of agency. A magical object had the same uncomposed efficacy as the act which struck fire from flint. All things were full of gods. Primitive man was not a fumbling intellectual entertaining a defective theory. Order in nature waited upon the order of deed and utterance. Pythagoras did geometry, and nature loomed in the mode of space. But nature is not the "great apparition"; it never was an apparition—an instant appearance. Indeed, an enduring frustration has marked the many attempts to reach "reality" from a basis of appearances. Nature is *ex post facto*. It vanishes in the abstract present tense. Magical objects are the reflection of the magical act. The order of nature, similarly, reflects the order of the *actual*. Any continuum resides in the actual, in the verb, in the *midworld,* never in passivity and its discrete and miraculous data.

The long disrepute of the universal is the consequence of the failure to have recognized universals as the shape, order, form, continuum of the incorporate actuality. The universal then seemed "pure thought," mental, ideal, psychic, divorced from *the* body, from the organism, from local control, from self-maintenance. Even today what we call the "organism" has remained mysterious. In scientific terms there is no organizing object, i.e., no local control. Biology has been an irritant to physics, and physics to biology. Physics does not speak of "adjustment" or of "adaptation" to an "environment" by stars, stones, or electrons. Biology retains a spooky quality. But nothing is more spooky than nature itself when regarded as a datum or apparition. As merely "there" and unaccountable it has the status of an apparition without connection with any control, very like a spook. To put the matter in blunt terms: I am proposing to rescue nature from that spooky status which it still occupies in so far as it is treated as an apparition, uncontrolled within itself and without generation. Short of an incorporate actuality of which nature is the material and formal continuum, nature has remained a spooky apparition, a phenomenon. It may be added that short of local control there is no history of physics because no evolution of its order.

Going to the post office, telling time, counting fingers, and in all ways identified in a verb, I have found old problems made plausible because their basis was passivity. I have felt respect for Berkeley because of his decent appeal to say what one could possibly mean by "matter." Berkeley found no matter as a psychological datum. Radical empiricism has never found any. I will say briefly that if one has any strong penchant for a material world one had better settle for the *functioning object* as its locus, for the organism, for yardsticks, clocks, balances, numerical notation, and for the word, for the eloquent utterance of any sort, and for their revelation. If matter be not constitutional then the philosopher has no business with it. Similarly, the denial of connections in Hume becomes a consequence of empirical passivity. Necessary connection is a tautology.

But such notable problems are not to be dismissed. They have had currency and authority. And then there was Kant, proposing to restore order to natural science but without yardsticks or clocks or other functioning objects as the source of projected order. What is the resulting "phenomenal" world if not a spooky apparition? Still, it was an ordered apparition as against the discrete unconnectedness of all alleged psychological data. Where all is empirical, no empirical inquiry has any basis, necessity, restraint, enforcement. Again, there has been a long-standing "problem of universals," a source of controversy in medieval times. One cannot shrug it off or get around it by argument. As the form of the actual, the universal becomes resident in the verb and so in the functioning object and its continuum. Philosophy has no necessary answers apart from necessary problems. But the equation of the present person with his intimate, necessary, and identifying problems has rarely been made or written.

But I have promises to keep and cannot keep them all. Perhaps others will elaborate the consequences of the actual in many other constitutional ways. I propose the actual as the neglected source of order and selfhood. It is a risk. But

> He either fears his fate too much
> Or his deserts are small
> Who will not put it to the touch
> To win or lose it all.

Nevertheless and for all that we are not likely to abandon the facts although admitting artifacts. Thoreau picks up an arrowhead at a place and time, at Concord, say. And that artifact is made from stone. Stones are among the facts, items in nature. On that basis we are required to accept them, as if nature imposed a control on the accreditation of any alleged fact. The familiar question "Is that a fact?" suggests criteria and so restraint, guardedness, responsibility, accountability. Strange that we should be accountable where we could exercise no personal control and may not do so. Whatever the facts may be has been regarded as quite out of our power to originate or modify. This has been a powerful persuasion. Had we such power over the region of facts, "would we not shatter it to bits and then remold it nearer to the heart's desire?" But desire has given hostages to the facts. In both its formulation and execution it assumed nature and then has sought to evade that dependency. The result, both East and West, has been a suspicion of desire itself, as in Stoicism, Buddhism. All is vanity. Abandon desire or patronize it as a deluded privacy.

The tenacity of the persuasion that the facts do concern us in utterance and other acts suggests that we have not been disposed to settle for their irrelevance, we proceeding on our untrammeled way. We take satisfaction in recognizing the facts, chide those who will not, and pity those who cannot. We do, we should, allow them some control. Responsible actions take them into account. But unless the facts are also constitutional to our deeds, our disregard entails no criticism, no charge of failure, nor censure of oneself by oneself. Ought one to take them into account although not a party to their authority? Admittedly we can be held responsible only for what we do. Unless the facts in their status and authority reflect and embody our doings they lose their command and tenacity. I am responsible for what I do only if the doing be itself the source and cause of my responsibility.

Certainly a sticky point, this alliance of command and action—that we cannot be *responsible to* when we are not also *a party to* what would command and control. This being "a party to" the facts and to nature suggests what I have been calling the *functioning object,* not a functional object, not a tool, not an instrument, nor a means to a specific and terminating satisfaction.

The functioning object is that immediacy which embodies the verb—organism, yardstick, clock, balance, number, word. Functioning objects are legislative. They are revelatory. They are not perceived. In the midworld projected by functioning objects we behold ourselves. "For the eye does not see itself but by reflection in other things," as Brutus says to Cassius. The Parthenon reveals the mind of Athens, its glory and its failure, as the Republic does for Rome. Primitive art reveals the primitive mind. History is not chronicle but rather the quest for the energies which found utterance in Chartres or the Magna Carta. In history we both exhibit and discover our energies and thereby ourselves. History is no spectator sport. If I rather drum on this point—on functioning objects and on the midworld—it is because in the opposition of appearance and reality I could find neither. Each cancels the other. Neither allows that local control of which the distinction between them is a consequence. Short of counting fingers or marbles I cannot make a mistake; short of going to the post office I cannot lose my way. Our common sense—the common and the universal—derive from the verb and the actual. A common sense has long been sought. The universal was a distinctive discovery of classical Greece. But it was divorced from any doing and so obliterated the agent and the individual. No one was authoritatively present, nor was any functioning object, *the* body, or the utterance. There was no midworld.

Berkeley had no eye for the reception of "the divine visual language"; Kant had no legislative yardstick or clock; Emerson was not "looking"—a verb—with his "transparent eyeball." The psychologist measures reaction time; he refers to a stop-watch; there is no clock nor any other legislative actuality in the stream of consciousness. In the absence of local control no one ever found a cause or an effect. Why seek the living within the alleged appearances or else in some reality which may not be among the appearances? Any negative advertises local control, and a threat to self-maintaining actuality. Why not "lose the name of action" if the actual be not the revelation of both world and individual?

10

The Ahistoric Ideal

I Mistrust of Time

A point of departure for a consideration of the idea of history occurs in the prevalence of the ahistoric temper. As Ortega has observed, our characteristic mode of thought is still Eleatic. It is a temper which finds the ideal of inquiry in permanence, in a substance or formula which remains fixed, which includes all change, perhaps explains it, or brings it under a rule of law. This inclusion of change in constancy has, indeed, appeared to many as the essential characteristic of reason. Multiplicity without unity has seemed the defeat of understanding. Change without order offers no distinction from chaos. Philosophy has, accordingly, been engaged in an escape from time which is the medium of change.

It is this ahistoric ideal which has stood in the way of bringing history into the domain of philosophy. Although history is the sole record of our actual fortunes it has seldom seemed to be capable of satisfying our hopes, whether moral or intellectual. All the transactions of history occur in time and have seemed to require a point of view outside of time for their fulfillment and for their understanding. Brutus says to Cassius "O Cassius, I am sick of many griefs," and has for answer, "Of your philosophy you make no use if you give way to accidental evils." To be "philosophical" requires, then, that we see accident and fortune circumvented. It requires us to seek identity with that reality, or with those powers, that reduce temporal triumph and disaster to equal unimportance. They are both imposters. Time and action become inadequate vehicles of our destiny. They obscure our timeless essence. Action occurs in circumstance which we do not fully control, and these circumstances seduce our wills to enterprises which are not only interminable and variable, but in principle distracting. One gives way to accidental evils not only in mourning misfortune, but in allowing unpleasant events to solicit one's energies at the outset. That is where the mistake was made. An ideal serenity would never find in time occasion for passionate and absorbing action. Brutus should never have become a devoted republican.

We have wanted to return to some ideal serenity. There we could "see life steadily and see it whole." The One would remain while the many changed and passed. Temporal fortunes, good or bad, would lose appeal and rejection when seen *sub specie aeternitatis,* in their eternal bearing. Such sentiments have been entertained by thoughtful men, by many who have pretended to morality and intelligence. Time is then superseded by the timeless, by permanence and law, and fortune embraced in a grand design which controls all events and is not controlled by them.

History, however, is all too plainly an affair of time. There kingdoms rise and wane. The recording angel takes note of our deeds and thoughts only in so far as they exhibit fidelity or treason to eternal law, since that is all that matters from his point of view. The historian, in contrast, tells of ephemeral transactions, important in time and there effective, even though they can be brought to no final assize. His kingdom is always of this world, and finality would abolish the spectacle which he contemplates and the enterprise in which he participates. The historical person leaves his mark on the vehicles of finitude, on institutions, states, art, science, and commerce. Action is the acknowledgment and exhibition of limit. The Constitution had hardly been adopted when it was promptly amended, and thereafter amended again. Nor would one care to say that the last word had been spoken. The assessment of the historical status of a man occurs apropos of such mutabilities. His contribution is to time and, in that medium, his most intense declarations and his most decisive deeds recede into a past where, because they are past, they no longer stand unmodified in a new present. A book on history is not the report of the secretary of the cosmos. Much is forgotten, much poorly known, and all understood with difficulty and, perhaps, misunderstood. It is notable that the "truth" about the past occurs only in inspired books claiming a competence not limited by time, and so not historical. When theories of history propose a general and supervisory view of all temporal transactions they suggest rather the other-worldly spectator than the finite participant in improvised deeds, adapted to the time, suitable for maintaining a precarious present. In so far as yesterday is like today we are not in history: we may be in eternity, or in an ecstacy, or in a haze, but we are not then in the region of things done.

The historical act stands in circumstance, but in a historical circumstance which is itself the residue of deeds. It is a continuation of discourse, an extension of what has already been said and done, a sequel to an enterprise already under way. The supposed act which does not emerge from heritage can find no lodgment there, and no reception in the record of historical education. Time is of its essence, and this quality brings forward its unorthodox status. It is the aspect of history which separates it from ahistoric modes of experience and from all types of truth expressed in the abstract present tense, as when one says that $7 + 5 = 12$. Historiography is the disclosure of the act in its temporal heritage, in its antecedent and consequent involvements.

Time has, indeed, seemed to be the destructive element. We have wanted to elude it and to stand in the timeless. In the procession of days one finds only what the rust and the moths will corrupt. Our lives are as the grass, and we have looked before and after and pined for what is not. *Eheu fugaces,* the fleeting years glide on, and even as we talk envious time is on the wing. Time is no revealer of absolute truth, and the light that is in us has seemed but a darkness. We aspire to advance *ex umbris et imaginibus in veritatem,* from shadows and illusions into truth. Plans and reputations pass into oblivion: "Look on my works, ye mighty, and despair." *"Hélas, et le bon roy d'Espaigne, duquel je ne scay pas le nom,"* not even the name, and he is a king. Noble and passionate desires find no scope and no fulfillment. Socrates thought that the wise man studies to die, to rid himself even now of perishable appetites, and so equip the soul to hold high converse with Minos and Rhadamanthus on the farther shore. At best we are such things as dreams are made of and, at worst, we play such fantastic tricks before high heaven as make the angels weep. Time has seemed a bankrupt. It seems a pensioner of the eternal, without assets of its own, debasing if taken seriously, an *ignis fatuus* for desire and a darkness for the mind.

It is, indeed, conservative to say that we have not found time altogether satisfactory. It does not quite suit us. We say we do not really belong there but out of its reach. Nor does that sentiment occur only in more poetic moods. Like other scholars, historians, or some of them, would like to know what "unity" informs the materials with which they deal. The historian deals in acts, in what has been said, expressed or done, of which a record has been left in a writing or other monument. It is no easy matter to make order out of the acts of a single individual, taking into account, too, that, since Freud, we are all a bit mad and badly put together even in our psychology. What hope, then, of finding unity in all the acts of all the men of whom some memento remains? It seems a preposterous proposal. But then, what is the alternative? Is it that acts are formless, vagrant, lawless, incapable of exhibiting an order in their very identification? This problem troubled Henry Adams. On leaving his teaching work at Harvard College he took stock of his own mind and of the effect of his instruction on students. What he saw was not encouraging. He says of the historian: "He makes of his scholars either priests or atheists, plutocrats or socialists, judges or anarchists, almost in spite of himself. In essence incoherent and im-

moral, history had either to be taught as such—or fal-
sified." And he adds: "For all serious purpose, it was less
instructive than Walter Scott or Alexander Dumas."

The misgivings of Adams are those of a man for whom
history was not merely an intellectual spectacle or a factual
chronology. It seems fair to say that in the shapes of the
past he saw an operative energy, something more than psychological because more than an essay in specific adjust-
ments. It was, indeed, as a vision of organization that
Chartres could hold his interest and command his enthusiasm. Here was energy of prodigious intensity taking shape
in a luminous lyricism. Chartres embodied a "serious purpose" objectified in a structure of enormous complexity
and composed unity. It was not disconcerting to the simple
man nor boring to the most sensitive and thoughtful. It
was no gadget, no device, no shrewd practical move. It
seems fair to say that Adams did not see history with finitude left out, nor yet as a finitude without the greatness and
the power of a composing universality. The enervated, the
flaccid, the lethargic could not build a Chartres, any more
than could the utilitarian. Like the dynamo, the Virgin was
a prime mover, and neither was comprehensible apart from
our identification with its allurements.

But how was one to make sense of both Virgin and dynamo? Energy is all very well, but does it lead only to corruptible and transient works? There is no new Chartres,
and Adams himself labored to clarify a faded mediaevalism
very alien to the Chicago Fair of 1893. And, after all, the
Parthenon is an eloquent building, too, and still glows with
the splendor of Athens. The polis has not lost all authority
to the later vision of "The City of God." It is in the presence of these diversities, these various and perhaps incoherent energies, that the impartial historian is tempted to recommend Sir Walter Scott. "Now who shall arbitrate; ten
men love what I hate." In 378 A.D. Quintus Arelius Sym-
machus, an old Roman and pagan, protested the removal
from the Senate house of a statue of Victory which had
long stood there as a symbol of the glory of Rome. But the
Bishop of Milan happened to be St. Ambrose, and he made

it plain to the Emperor that if he valued the political loyalty of Christians he would do well to have no altar to Victory. One was not to have visions of Proteus rising from the sea or hear old Triton blow his wreathed horn.

History includes all sorts. If there is to be a place for Augustine there will be one for Pelagius. "Caesar had his Brutus, Charles the First his Cromwell." What is to prevent the student from finding something attractive in Pelagius? The student of history is doomed to read the *Communist Manifesto* as well as the Declaration of Independence, Immanuel Kant as well as John Locke. Nor were the middle ages fully expressed in "storied windows, richly dight, casting a dim religious light": there was also the sack of Constantinople in 1204 by the devout soldiery of the Fourth Crusade. One can understand why Adams found history incoherent and immoral and hardly the place to reveal the serious purpose of life. Intellectually, it seems a region without intrinsic system and, morally, it makes no firm and final recommendations.

The Eleatic ideal expressed and served the intellect. It has never been abandoned for all its permutations in substances one or many, in atoms, the soul, the Absolute, in causality and formulated regularities, or even in its more recent expressions as unqualified sense data, atomic facts, and sets of postulates which are valid in all possible worlds. All these have been powerful proposals. They are often at odds with each other. Even the intellectuals have grown weary of the strife and now they capitulate by proposing nothing more robust than the study of word usage. One might think that it is in the dictionary that one discovers how, in fact, words have been used, how they are now used. But use, it turns out, is not enough, for, it is alleged, some words are misused. The criterion for misuse is always some supposed pattern of propriety regarded as something other than actual usage, something more solid and fundamental than current speech, or, indeed, than any speech.

But none of these proposals makes time of the essence. None is identified through a date as an essential element in the discovery of its meaning. They all serve the ahistoric ideal. With action and with history the case is otherwise. There time is of the essence, and this feature is the mark of its intellectual unorthodoxy. Never send to know of the historian any timeless truth. He will tell you, perhaps a bit wryly, that such and such a person believed that he had circumvented time, but as historian he will not say that the attempt had succeeded, or even that it had failed. He will not even say, as a rule, that his own story, or the stories of Herodotus, Gibbon, or Ranke are past amendment, or that the writing of history—any more than the deeds which history records—can elude the influences of a particular time. For time, and dates, embrace all that is done, pervade and identify all that is done, not excluding historiography itself. The intellectual ideal, still dominant, appears with Brutus, sick of many griefs and eager to evade accidental evils in an untroubled constancy. The aim is to set us right. Well, Henry Clay said he would rather be right than President. Very likely the two are mutually exclusive, somewhat to the consternation of Eleatic moralists.

Perhaps it is possible now to suggest in a preliminary way that it is no easy matter to attach oneself to the processes of time. Among philosophers—and they are the ones who study the constitution of experience—finitude has never been a "category," i.e., a factor in the verb "to be." In Conrad's *Lord Jim* the wise old counsellor Stein advises that the broken Jim lose himself in some actuality: "In the destructive element immerse." Jim was to relinquish his romantic dreams and his enfeebling drift by joining some demanding society, giving loyalty, and receiving it. Only so, said Stein, could he pull himself together and act effectively in the dubious battles of a concrete imperfection. How fully Jim took this advice is a nice question. "He was one of us," said Marlowe in a moving epitaph; but his lady-love said that he was false.

Idealism has more appeal than is usually supposed, and the acceptance of limitation much less. Without the ideal, particulars seem disintegrative, the will lost in impulse, reason bewildered in opinion, the imagination captivated by fantasy. It is not too much to say that the universal and timeless draws its primary compulsion not from its other-worldliness, but from its capacity to make sense of the here and now, endowing objects and acts with order and, in that flash of understanding, establishing the difference between a shadowy consciousness and a structured objectivity. It is a great advance when one has found oneself able to make a mistake, but the price of error is some pretention to an objective order in experience. This alone can put impulse, opinion, and fantasy in their places. It alone can identify them. They occur in the assertion and maintenance of a formal structure.

In primitive societies action is ritualistic. Ritual is the apparatus for lifting an unorganized immediacy into a new status of connection with a stable power and a non-subjective reality. The Etruscans are said to have introduced augury to Rome. The flight of birds indicated the sanction of the gods. Grace before meat serves to heighten the actuality of eating by putting one's dinner in an environment and abating an animal voracity. Formulae delay the impulsive (see W. E. Hocking, *Human Nature and its Remaking*). Revolt from formula is perennial, but when this revolt becomes a general denial of propriety it degenerates into the slovenly and insignificant. Formulae tend to become ahistoric and fixed, but their original function was to heighten, sharpen, and enliven the moment rather than to obliterate or disqualify it. They become demonic, as Paul Tillich points out in an early work, *The Interpretation of History*. The ahistoric temper carries, however, such axiomatic enticement as to send us looking for a new and better formula. The actual, in consequence, never acquires authority of its own, and it cannot do so until infinity, i.e., order, becomes the form of finitude, and finitude the actuality of the infinite. But this is difficult. Like Lord Jim, we tend to run out on the actual, looking for the "right" moment and so, of course, never finding it. But where any actual situation is devoid of finality, all finality vanishes so that the very idealism which seemed fortifying and integrative loses its concrete occasions. Then we hear only the melancholy, long, withdrawing roar of the sea of faith.

II The Ahistoric in Plato

The suspicion of time, and the quest for the immutable where there is no change or shadow of turning, has deep roots in philosophy. An example may be taken from Plato. On the day after Socrates and some friends had talked politics, presumably the dialogue of *The Republic,* there was further conversation, this time about cosmology, the structure and the genesis of nature. This sequent dialogue is the *Timaeus.* It has been an influential book and was put in Plato's hand by Raphael in the Vatican painting "The School of Athens." Timaeus says in a well-known passage: "The city and citizens which you yesterday described to us in fiction we will now transfer to the world of reality." He then proceeds in high vein: "First, then, we must make a distinction and ask, 'What is that which always is and has no becoming, and what is that which is always becoming and never is?' That which is apprehended by intelligence and reason is always in the same state, but that which is conceived by opinion, with the help of sensation, and without reason, is always in the process of becoming and perishing, and never really is."

The Republic could qualify as no better than a "fiction" unless it could draw authority from a world we never made, from the nature of things. The just state needed to reflect the values embodied in the cosmos. It was an arrangement of finite affairs which would stimulate the cultivated class to a concern with the purely good and rational. The unjust state would not do this. It would be no more than an invitation to delusive egoism, to the triumph of the stronger, or the aggrandizement of the prudent, the circumspect, and the conventional. Plato wanted a justice beyond opinion and change so that it would lose no reality, nor any authority, "whether seen or unseen by gods or by men." Aristotle says that Plato saw "all sensible things in a state of constant flux" and that, consequently, "we can have no knowledge of them." (*Metaphysics,* Chapter IX, assembles twenty-three objections to the theory of ideas.) Whatever "really is" needs to stand outside of time. It is to be identified without benefit of date. Plato did not say that human reason was bankrupt, but only that the price of solvency was alliance with ahistoric essences. Not the least manifestation of Plato's monumental distincton occurs in his later misgivings over a rationality which loses its articulation in the absolute unity of pure Being.

Without the support of the primordial realities described in the *Timaeus* the arrangements of *The Republic* seemed only a fiction. We may, with the positivists, reject all such metaphysical sanctions as nothing better than the rationalization of desire. If we do, we have to admit that the works of such rationalized faith are prodigious. One needs to be careful not to prove too much. Actual men, identified historically through dates, did support their institutions and utter their works of art under the influence of ahistoric ideals. Impulse may be aroused by a passing condition, but enduring and thoughtfully sustained energies have reflected the stability of magnetic and minatory finalities. The much-devising Odysseus had a friend in the gray-eyed Athena. But what we might today call the scientific temper, of which Plato had his share, proposed the constancies of geometry and reason. They seemed to be not so much objects of subjective consciousness as its form and force.

From this sense of informing permanence sprang the conviction of finitude. Despair of time is not dissatisfaction with a particular. "That was o'erpassed; this may pass also." Finitude is no less a formal and systematic idea than infinity and it acquired no importance until an orderly and ideal structure within itself gave it an arresting actuality. It isn't so much that only the uncouth regard the mind or the soul as an entity and then elaborately demonstrate its existence or its non-existence. It is rather that, on that basis, the mind or the soul were neither discovered nor proposed. For all the incompleteness and lack of finality of its content, the mind had importance as the locus of formal procedures. Plato saw it that way in the *Phaedo*. Every outer infinity reflects the form of finitude, and no outer infinity appeared with conviction until finitude itself became ideal. *The Republic* without the *Timaeus* may have seemed a fiction, but it was no patchwork and no vagrancy. *The Republic* is a fiction of the same sort as any artful composition. Its alternative was not fact, as opposed to fiction, but the degeneration of the citizen into subjective anarchy. The tensions inherent in the problem of actualizing justice mark at the same time the ideality of both the finite and the infinite.

The Absolute was called by Hegel "the lion's cave to which all foot tracks lead and from which none return." He had a point. Still it could be observed that discovering a lion's cave where there were no footprints would make lions even more mysterious. What is worse, his alleged victims become rather strange too, if their footprints could suddenly vanish without cause. On the most conservative hypothesis one is forced to say that nobody would know about the lion if there were no footprints leading to his cave. But if *all* go there it begins to look as if no other ground for identifying them were known. Points of no return lose their monopoly of mystery, however, when they depend for their discovery on the urgency which brings us to them. Of course Hegel was quite aware of this. It is a consideration, however, which may permit one to sympathize with Plato's urgency to reach the primordial. It was no escapism, though it became so as the classical temper weakened, and the actual lost its intrinsic authority.

The ahistoric is always characterized by purity. It is a condition purged of finitude and of its modes of actuality. It is represented as free from error, problems, and specific affections. In *The Symposium* Plato speaks of the "lesser mysteries of love" with a good deal of approval and admiration. The lover is agent, generator, creator. He is parent, artist, and statesman. Full approval, however, is reserved for the greater mysteries, and these concern the charm of "beauty absolute, separate, simple, and everlasting." In that unsullied perfection there is no growth or decay. It does not occur in a bodily frame or "in any form of speech or knowledge." It is not "clogged with pollutions of mortality." Yet one can overplay this note. Love was also the child of Poverty and Plenty, begotten in an oblivious debauch. If the philosopher studies to die he—as Socrates—awaits more splendid talk when untroubled by the cares of bodily existence. "One could do worse than be a swinger of birches." One is hard put to it to allege that the timeless has nothing at all to do with the actual, that it is altogether remote, separate, irrelevant. The Absolute is no respecter of persons, but neither was the Absolute discovered without self-respect.

Modern polemicists give the impression that the Absolute, Plato's or another's, is an intellectual hypothesis, which, being out of empirical reach, is no better than nonsense. It was not such a hypothesis in its historical occasion. It was rather a consequence of a sense of finitude, and it was pre-eminently an essay in the preservation of that intensity. For, as noted, finitude is not a fact. Like infinity it is everywhere. It has no color, shape, specific gravity, or coefficient of expansion. It is an intensity, an energy, and it has to be maintained. Not to maintain it is collapse or madness. This is the setting for the discovery of the ahistoric. We are quite familiar with the orthodoxy which sees evil and error as a disregard of the ideal; we are not so well acquainted with the complementary consideration that evil and error appear as the relinquishment of finitude. In *Major Barbara,* Barbara complained of the incessant begging for money, something she would never do for herself. Her father remarks ironically, "Genuine unselfishness is capable of anything, my dear." Machiavelli observes, "For how we live is so far removed from how we ought to live that he who abandons what is done for what ought to be done will rather bring about his own ruin than his preservation." The great Florentine spoke practically, yet desperately too, but his words have a larger application. Shall we say that what ought to be done, or thought, obliterates occasions or, rather, that, lacking occasion, the ideal is itself unintelligible, an escape from reason and from every exhibition of the living moment? Utopia began as an essay in saving occasions. When this is forgotten both the actual and the ideal lose articulation.

III The Ahistoric in Boethius

A further and celebrated instance of temporal misgivings occurs in *The Consolation of Philosophy* of A. M. S. Boethius. This little book has been widely translated, commented upon, and imitated. Its author was a scholar, a Roman consul, and minister to the Visigothic master of Italy, Theodoric the Great. One would not choose it for originality, but rather for its enduring influence. Boethius died fifty years after the collapse of the Western Empire, at the end of the classic period and the beginning of the Middle Ages. Five years later Justinian closed the University of Athens and St. Benedict founded his monastery at Monte Casino. It was a transitional century.

Charged with treason, Boethius had been thrown into prison by Theodoric. There he contemplated the ruin of his personal ambitions and his prospective execution. How was he to understand a fortune so variable and so harsh? As he tells the story his first spiritual refuge was with the Muses who so often in the past had brought him delight. But now his situation was serious and he exclaims, "Why, O my friends, did ye so often puff me up, telling me that I was fortunate? For he that is fallen low never did firmly stand." Lady Philosophy appears, fiercely dismisses the Muses: "Who has suffered these seducing mummers to approach this sick man?" one, moreover, "nourished in the lore of the Eleactics and Academics" and therefore in need of a more astringent therapy. She then leads Boethius to contemplate and assess temporal values—wealth, status, honor, power—declaring that complaint about the ways of a world which paid in such counterfeit coin was hardly suitable. One ought, rather, to discern in present distress the hand of chastisement and the voice of instruction. An all-inclusive Providence subordinates time to a poised serenity in which personal fortune is transfigured. "What we should rightly call eternal is that which grasps and possesses wholly and simultaneously the fullness of unending life, which lacks naught of the future and has lost none of the fleeting past." The alternative to change and fortune is found in the ahistoric. In that constancy all events are under control or, rather, none is out of control. In alliance with that perfection the turbulence of ambition is stilled and rebellion gives way to acceptance. Strictly speaking, the future has ceased to exist. "If you would weigh the foreknowledge by which God distinguishes all things, you will more rightly hold it to be a knowledge of a never-failing constancy in the present than a foreknowledge of the future." Job heard the voice of the whirlwind and laid his hand upon his mouth; but Boethius listened to the reasoned words of Lady Philosophy which echoed the voice within his own mind. Job stayed outside omnipotence; Boethius declared his own nature allied with it. For that reason the status of time is brought within our own appraisal.

If time ever had any attraction it was only because of our own identification with it; when it lost authority the self which had been identified with it was also rejected, and by its own reflective labors. The power of the ahistoric was not disclosed by means of a fact, or through an arbitrary and remote reality, but rather in a promise to integrate our own thought and to satisfy our wills. Job's vision of omnipotence was not, strictly, a perception of the ahistoric ideal. He saw only a powerful reality, but not the organizational ideal of finitude itself. Job never admitted that his way of life merited ill fortune. The exhortations of his friends left him unmoved. Boethius saw that he was getting only what he had coming to him—not quite the same as one's deserts. Job was overpowered by a fact; Boethius by an ideal of organized living. For these reasons, Job is the more primitive conception, deficient in self-consciousness. His problem was posed on terms which Elea and Athens had made no longer applicable. Indeed, our heritage perpetuates this pre-ahistoric conception of facts and forces. The question of the status of history was not, however, raised until the ahistoric had become the accepted destiny of thoughtfulness. The problem of an ahistoric absolute was not proposed on the basis of experience which, like Job's, was only psychological. Until we had declared an alliance with fortune we could not weigh its adequacy and thereupon betake ourselves to the ahistoric stability. Job, it seems, liked flocks and herds. He is not represented as suspicious of such satisfactions, or as being aware of the deficiency of self-consciousness which they imply. Nor did his friends suggest, as did Lady Philosophy to Boethius, that his mistake lay in wanting prosperity. In the sequel he prospered again and was content.

The ahistoric absolute develops from personal urgency rather than from the properties of objects. For this reason it can be neither proposed nor defended by argument. And so its wide success, wherever men have been both thoughtful and active, has often seemed intellectually outrageous, and a mark of superstition or of darkness. It lacks the calm impersonality of atomic sense-data and the non-involvement of the hypothesis where, with equal poise, one finds balm or bane in Gilead. To find it plausible one must participate in its derivation and so in the personal demand which launches it. An attack on a man's absolutes is an attack on the man, not on his discrete experiences. The same considerations which throw suspicion on finalities strike at the individual who needs them for the authentication of his own energies, i.e., of his own actuality, his efficacy, his place in the world. Selfhood may bring distortion and vast misunderstanding. But we purchase finitude only at the price of infinities which reveal the conception of the self with which we are identified.

The self is not made finite by objects because it is not found there. Its finitude is systematic, the other side of its systematic ideal. One does not come upon finitude as a "fact," but as an organization which controls even what one will take as a fact rather than as an appearance, error, or illusion. As we change absolutes we change ourselves and the world. These changes constitute history. History is the story of the transformations of absolutes. The infinite has the paradoxical quality of setting limits to persons and rescuing them from an incessant and endless variety. To propose the absolute is to discover the finite. To reject the absolute because it is not "verifiable"—and it is not—is to lose finitude as well as infinity. "The intellectual" is under some suspicion, and understandably so, when his own words and deeds invoke no systematic overthrow. "Whom God deigns not to overthrow hath need of triple brass."

All absolutes are doomed, but not by the intellect which cannot so much as propose them. They are doomed by history which is the process which reveals them and so overpasses any one of them, and all of them. It takes time. Historians, not excluding historians of philosophy, have not accepted time as a category. And so we have "theories" of history, all of which are wrong. The proposal of an absolute marks the discovery of the finite. The static absolute is the obliteration of the finite. History is the preservation of the finite in the revision of self-defining absolutes. The authority of time derives from the dated actuality which it receives in the revision of ahistoric idealizations. Apart from that process time remains a phenomenon, irrelevant to the energies of men, irrelevant to their finitude. That is why so great a man as Kant had, at last, to look for the compulsions of will in an abstract moralism. In the *Symposium* Alcibiades' entrance interrupts the light-hearted discourse on love and when he too makes his contribution it is to point to Socrates himself as the embodiment and actuality of that aspiration of which Diotima had spoken. So too, we may point to the *Critique of Pure Reason* as the product of that moral energy which made 1781 a date in the history of western self-consciousness.

The inquiring mind has, at times, banked on a rational world, one which will furnish answers to suitable questions and so endow questions with authority. But if one makes a point of this and declares that "the real is the rational," one has stepped out of logical bounds into egoism, into an ideal actuality which proclaims an alliance with an infinite object. Then one has joined Boethius in proposing a world which takes one's personal requirements into account.

IV The Ahistoric in Augustine

A third and celebrated example of ahistoric unity occurs in Augustine. Plato tried to give authority to the government of a city-state, Boethius looked for assurance in the midst of private calamity, and Augustine attempted a restoration of confidence when the capture of Rome by the Goths brought confusion to the Empire of the West. In his *Confessions,* as well as in *The City of God,* one finds a more deliberate objectification of time, and of man in time, than occurs in Plato or Boethius. He was a man of unsurpassed intensity and he stood at a moment of history when the greatest political achievements were being overthrown by barbarians who, though Christian, were also Arian heretics.

Under such circumstances one needed a remedy commensurate with the disaster. No destiny for man in his temporal exertions could be imagined on the basis of any visible assurances which the earthly city could supply. One must bear in mind, too, the fierce egoism of Augustine, whose conversion was no weak-minded acceptance of a facile and sentimental bliss, but the consequences of resolution and ardors such as few men can endure. Such a man, in such a time, could settle for nothing less than a view which both validated his lonely insurgency and reconciled him to a distracted world through an objective reality as absolute as his own egoism. Time and all it contains became creatures of the timeless. "For that very time did'st Thou make, nor could time pass by before Thou madest those times. But, if before Heaven and Earth there was no time, why is it demanded what Thou then did'st! For there was no 'then' when there was no time" (*Confessions,* Book XI). He says that in the eternal "nothing passeth, but the whole is present, whereas no time is all at once present." Similar statements occur in *The City of God:* "His knowledge is not as ours is, admitting alteration by circumstance of time, but exempted from all change and variations of moments; for His intention runs not from thought to thought; all things

He knows are present at the same time in His spiritual vision" (Book XI).

Although Augustine precedes Boethius by a century his subordination of time to the eternal is Christian rather than classical and therefore carries forward into the later thought of the Western world. Besides recognizing the divine governance of all creatures his views include and require a progressive intervention of the eternal in the events of time. He did not agree with Solomon that there was nothing new under the sun. Above all there had been the events of the Incarnation and of the Redemption. Time, although lost in the invariant, came to possess a status of a new sort. It was not illusory, for the Word had been made flesh and dwelt among us. A single reality embraced both earth and heaven, so that the affairs of earth were no longer pale shadows of unchanging essences nor merely comprehended in a divine omniscience. They had a status of their own so that the will of God might, or might not, be done in earth as in heaven. In Eden the divine governance was allegedly a fact; in Hippo it became an experience. As experience it required the Fall, the inheritance of original sin, and the sense of personal sin, so that the fact would be forever displaced by the experience of alienation and redemption. Much emphasis has been placed upon the Fall, and rightly, for it resulted from an act which was not God's but man's. Yet this act, the rival of God, left a world which no act could master. Egoism began as an estrangement and Augustine, who knew a great deal about it, could not relinquish it without losing his own energetic self; nor yet could he abide with it as sufficient for the peace which he so desperately wanted as only the egotist can.

The idea of history in systematic form stems from Augustine. It became a systematic idea when there appeared not only the opposition of the many and the one, or of fortune and its providential control, but the alliance of time with the absolute by means of action. History deals with acts not with thoughts detached and contemplative, except as they lead to something done. It is in the act that we make mistakes and in mistakes that we see the difference between

ourselves and our world. But there was no act until something done became an absolute, and it did not do that until
it somehow unsettled, or somehow sustained, both the self
and its world. Augustine was dealing with no specific frustration, with no maladjustment to his sensible environment. He was, rather, appalled by a threat to the possibility
of his own egoism. He proposed to be of some account,
even here upon this bank and shoal of time. The Church,
then, was the vehicle of his temporal worth, for it was the
kingdom of God on Earth; but it was the Church Militant,
and in that activity it was no phenomenon, no illusion, no
fact, but an enterprise shared by the human will in alliance
with the divine. Until the Fall no act had been performed.
Until then the finite lacked actuality. The very first attempt
at independence met severe rebuke. It seems that to know,
or to wish to know, the difference between good and evil is
to offend the God of *Genesis*. There has been no general or
authoritative dissent from the story of the Fall. Had it been
merely a question of an apple one might regard the punishment as not supported by enlightened views on penology.
Or even for disobedience a milder corrective with, perhaps, a bit of instruction, would seem more normal and
proportionate to the petty larceny. Not even the explanation that the act was committed against majestic omnipotence seems adequate. An earthly monarch, precarious in
power, might well, on occasion, find serious menace in a
violation of orders. But the creator of the whole world was
in no such perilous uncertainty. What had happened in
Eden was the appearance of a systematic rival to God,
namely, an act, and a human wish to know good and evil
for itself. To judge one's own acts is the same as acting. But
there lay the fatal rivalry, one which persists to our day.
The fascination and the truth of this story have nothing to
do with apples. It fascinates because the act is all that we can
call our own, all that is ourselves. Although the penalty was
harsh it has not been challenged in its basic propriety. A
person seems to us axiomatically capable of self-will; and
while we fear independence and, like God, cast the original
man out of the paradise of organization, we are equally sus-

picious of men who lack initiative and of societies who suppress it.

This, in short, is the problem of the "freedom of the will" and it is inherent in the pretention to have acted. It is central to the idea of history. It is in Augustine, not in Plato, Aristotle, or Boethius that this problem first gains formulation. To be "saved" means thereafter to act, not to have ideas, in tune with the universe. It is this dilemma which plagued Augustine and his successors. The act could not be abandoned nor yet, in view of its pretentions to autonomy, could it be accepted. Even to act "rightly" is to act "wrongly" if one alleges that the judgment is one's own and the motive one's own. Rather than have acts, and so finite autonomy, many philosophers have tried to get rid of acts altogether. This is one evidence of the failure of finitude and of history to become accredited categories. The verb "to be" does not include them. In this respect much recent philosophy is analogous to the pre-Augustinian intellectualism. It is not only ahistoric but anti-historic. And this consideration needs to be fastened upon if history is to become accredited or, more conservatively, if it is so much as to be examined as a constitutional element of our experience. The Fall may be deplorable in an abstract way, but when hearts have been lifted up and men have sung "Gloria in excelsis Deo," when Giotto painted the heavenly congregation around the throne, there seems no repining over the events which made possible the great revelation.

V The Skeptical Origin of the Ahistoric

The ahistoric, when deliberate, has a skeptical origin. Its force is that of the deep hesitation which it overcomes and its tenacity reflects the loss of orientation which its questioning would inflict. It is preceded by the naive and succeeded by the dogmatic. Our attitude toward it is ambiguous. Nobody wishes to be naively credulous, and yet no one can wish to be disturbed in his assurances. When so disturbed by others we may become resentful and take measures of censorship and repression. The skeptic reminds us of the insecurity of our own position and implies for us an arbitrariness, or a victimization, which is repugnant to our confidence and self-respect. The ahistoric derives its quality of "being" or of being "real" from the existential egoism of the skeptical experience. It is finitude which in one form or another troubles the skeptic, and it is infinity which in one form or another abates his frustration. Skepticism is arrest of function, not primarily arrest of thought. It is an inwardness of energy which can find no warrant for its exercise. The Platonic city needed the sanction of the nature of things. The sufferings of Boethius were not to be dismissed, but were to find propriety in Providence. The burning passions of Augustine required to be made pure in an absolute cause. The intellectual curiosity of Descartes found warrant in the consideration that God was no "deceiver," but stood as guarantor of both his own sharp finitude and of the world probed by his inquiries.

Hesitant men who do not take the plunge often seem deficient in force. Dante speaks of those who took no sides, "They were for themselves," and he saw the shadow of one who had made the great refusal, *"il gran rifiuto."* Montaigne preferred his tower to the bloody embroilments of the religious wars. Erasmus wrote: "I have always wished to be alone, and there is nothing I hate so much as sworn partisans." In his time there was no lack of partisanship. There seemed to him great need for a more equable humanity devoted to *bonae litterae*. Sir Thomas More lost his head and Erasmus remarked, "Would More had never meddled with that dangerous business and left the theological cause to the theologians." There is a greater and a lesser egoism, and, in the day of the "organization man," who will cast the first stone? For men who stand aside, when they are truly oppressed by fanatical crudity, have in their own measure affirmed a need of independence. And we owe to Erasmus the *Praise of Folly* with its playful but earnest presentation of a spontaneity deep in the core of all that is gentle and disinterested.

In so far as the ahistoric has this deliberate quality it discloses a practical rather than an intellectual origin. One is not in the most graceful posture when arguing an absolute, either up or down. In the end there is no tentative solution, but a weight of assurance which crushes any alleged substructure of hypothesis. Skepticism itself has no logical rationale. One is not argued into it or out of it. It is not a mistake which falls within an accredited discourse, or a truth for which evidence can be submitted. It is an experience, not a theory. It is a negative absolutism, but it is not nihilism, the interpretation of experience without any center of existence. The pervasiveness of intellectualism is illustrated by the criticism made of Descartes that he should have concluded *ergo quid est* rather than *ergo sum*. This is equivalent to not having Descartes there in the first place. He was there, however, in terms of a problem that took time. It was what he had been that made him what he became. His being did not rest on his consciousness of a doubt, but on a self-consciousness which carried a past into the disturbed present. There are no doubts in the present tense alone, nor any assurances either. Skepticism exhibits historical and practical traits in the mode of its appearance. Our age is anti-metaphysical because it lacks skepticism. Metaphysics of the transcendent sort baffles empirical and logical processes and leads to such epithets as "pseudo-concepts." A. J. Ayer has great respect for the "observations" which would lead one to accept a proposition as true. As an example of "the kind of utterance" which is no better than "nonsensical" he cites the assertion "that the world of sense-experience was altogether unreal." No possible way of showing this statement—or apparent statement—to be true or false could be proposed. It is "literally nonsensical" (*Language, Truth and Logic,*—an excellent and well-known treatment of epistemology untouched by skepticism.). If one attends to the circumstances of such utterances one finds no suggestion that the criterion of reality—or the idea of reality—was supposed to be discoverable among the particulars of "observation." One finds, rather, uneasiness over the status of observation, and this not because one's eyesight was failing or one's spectacles needed adjustment, but rather because ob-

servation seemed to possess inherent defects for the motives which led to its use. John Locke asked about the "origin" of human knowledge, a curious problem if one had
only one's senses to trust, or even one's senses plus the
tautologies of mathematics and, allegedly, of logic. He
asked about the "certainty and extent" of our knowledge,
questions of no "literal significance" in terms of qualities or
patterns of qualities. Locke, as a partial skeptic whose
books have had wide attention for nearly three centuries,
was interesting to people who wondered how they stood
with nature. Like true skeptics they were egoists. In
America the critical realists drew heavily on Locke, con-
cluding with him that much of what they saw in nature was
psychological rather than objectively independent of being
perceived. They felt that a man would be naive to suppose
that what he saw could be forthwith attributed to an independent nature. This story is familiar and need be only
named to summon up many actual and historical misgivings about the observed scene. Philosphy in looking for
knowledge has been moved by the same concerns which
operate morally, namely, does it come under our control or
not? Perhaps it does not. Perhaps the real is whatever it
happens to be quite apart from what one may suppose. The
denial of the ontological proof has been quite general: don't
read off the fact from the experience. In all these situations
the essential feature of skepticism reappears, namely, a demand for a view of experience which, like the wheel of fortune of Boethius, does not leave us unrelated to some stable
finality. Skepticism, to repeat, is the arrest of function. No
such arrest can be discovered in the positivistic approach.
The skeptic comes to reality, as do the various idealists, and
some realists, not apropos of ideas, but rather because of
the problem with which he is identified as a thoughtful
man. He has a past, not a past of shifting sense qualities, but
one that made large and exciting proposals about his own
finitude. It is out of this actuality that the ahistoric has
arisen. This, of course, in no way supports the ahistoric as
a final doctrine in the history of philosophy. It is only to
say that what appears in philosophy is to be viewed histori-

cally. Nor are the positivists to be excluded. They make it clear enough that on the terms proposed by tautologies and observation nothing historical can be so much as understood. This is no small contribution.

Philosophers have wanted to be "right" and to come into possession of an innocent truth. One of the chief attractions of history lies in its including mistakes and finitude. There time is of the essence, and so too the transformations which mark a past and its sequent present. The egoist, and he alone, takes possession of time. For others it is a phenomenon, a fact of the environment or a psychological datum. For a historical orientation it is no disgrace to have been wrong. On the contrary, it is an essential. To have been wrong invokes the past tense. Nobody is wrong in the static. Modern philosophy, influenced by physics rather than by history, has put on a determined search for the cognitively infallible. Since there is no present king of France it is plain that to say "The present king of France is bald" requires us to reduce or "analyse" that statement into its elements. There, in those elements, one will sooner or later come upon the "atomic facts" and stand in all intellectual probity. In the cognitive atom is no skepticism, no egoism, no dogmatism, no history. This interesting and remarkable performance has had considerable influence,not so much because anyone believes that "France" is an idea generated from sense data alone without benefit of history, but rather because it is an argument which catches philosophers where they are vulnerable. They have been, largely, subscribers to the cult of innocence and have wanted an epistemological paradise with no snake tempting us to know the difference between the true and false, or the good and the evil. St. Patrick, one reads, drove serpents from Ireland, Carnap and Schlick drove them out of Vienna, and, since Russell and Wittgenstein, none is left in Cambridge. Perhaps it is best not to shun the historical. It gives to man the opportunity for fame, i.e., for identification, for setting a date. But for this there is a price which truth cannot pay alone. A bit of error is also necessary. There is, indeed, another innocence, the sort that Plato found in enthusiasm, Augustine in holiness, and Erasmus in the praise of folly. Thrassa, the house-maid of Thales, did not fall into a well; but, then, she has bequeathed no reputation in astronomy. She has her repute as a sensible person who looked where she was going. It seems probable that she would know whether or not the king of Lydia was bald. No doubt there was gossip then, as now.

Skepticism was the first "pure" act of finitude. It is an utterance purely formal, devoid of factual content, yet actual and dependent on a past, on other and previous utterances. Like all that is historical it occurred as a definitive part of a temporal continuum. It is a position identified through time and it gave to time and to dates their first objectification based, as it is, on artifact, and not on fact. Upon it rest our ahistoric assurances and the claims of their propriety. Like skepticism, assurance occurs only as an utterance, not as content of passive experience. Had no pre-skeptical assurance been proposed, no truth asserted, no justice proclaimed—then the skeptical temper had not found its occasion. Its occasion is not data nor yet postulates, but articulate claims which neither data nor postulates can define. Skepticism mistrusts beliefs only because it mistrusts the men who have proposed them. Santayana asks how a picture of the universe could descend into the twilight of animal mind "beset by countless passions and lost in the infinite world which bore it." The assurances and the mistrust of assurances are alike our own and are neither supplied nor questioned by any content of consciousness. And so, the skeptic is no vagrant in a secure world, no oddity in a patent reality which he pathologically fails to accept, no phenomenon of cognitive neutrality. His address is to actuality, to what has been said and formalized, and for that reason to an expression of order and control. Skepticism is the prelude to respect for expression. It is the expression which takes note of expression. Consequently it underlies whatever may be said about symbols and their ontological force.

Skepticism is disinterested. This is not for the reason that it wants nothing at all, but because it wants an orderly and responsible view. Any answer which preserves criticism will appear to it as having merit. A good test of its worth lies in proposing criticism in its absence, before formal judgments in their various modes have been made, identified, and called into question. To such untested assurance one is not a party, and if one does make oneself a party to assurance one has before one the record of the distressful sequel to that essay. The disinterested is not the uninterested, where nothing satisfies and nothing offends, so that one could turn away without loss and entertain one's unconcern with other matters equally irrelevant to egoistic requirements. The disinterested occurs as a systematic finitide, tenacious of its conditions. It does not occur in abdication.

The existentialist literature, likewise concerned with the ego, presents it as anguished and forlorn, cut off from organization, alone in an empty privacy, and without an avowed and essential temporal record of its own deeds. Why the fuss about order and "essence" unless they are our own work, our own saying, in which we see what we are, so that their repudiation commits a suicide? Then, indeed, is one anguished and forlorn, empty, strained, and without either outer or inner invitation. The skeptical negativism, however, has not abandoned actuality and is nothing without it. It rests on society, on what has been said, and on its own utterances. Its insecurity is articulate and so volitionally grounded. It invokes the artifactual, not the real, and not a "Being" aloof from the concrete conditions of selfhood and of nature. It forces attention upon time, although not yet reconciled to time. Its uncertainty is infinite, but it is not apart from the formalities, including time itself, which define it and give it occasion. An orderly world is wanted. This is the grandeur of the skeptic as compared with the anxiety of, say, Kierkegaard objecting to "the" system or to any system, and so shrunken into the morbidity of a vanishing selfhood. Will one visit the deer park? "Do I dare to eat a peach?" It seems fair to say, then, that the disinterested desire springs from the disinterestedness of skeptical egoism. We crave a free functioning and the activity which, though essentially finite and temporal, stands in itself as its own warrant, projecting the world which it entails.

In wishing to be right we have overlooked the importance of being neither right nor wrong as a preliminary to either condition. It has rather seemed that we must start from the right in principle, and from truth unquestioned, in order to be thereafter right in detail. For this reason we have had self-evident truths, innate ideas, eternal verities, atomic facts, and much else. These are the historical monuments of the evasion of the skeptical position. They have their own fascination in a context that has not found time a category. They lack tense and are devised in a temper which seeks the timeless. We are to take them, not approve of them, either in detail or in principle. Thought cannot be found in what is imposed upon it, and so no egoism haunts these truly "primitive" ideas. Thought, indeed, has sought truth rather than freedom, and while the problem of the "freedom of the will" entices every neophyte, the equally basic and entailed problem of the freedom of thought is quashed by psychology and by the epistemology of passivity. In the main, time has seemed an obstacle to assurance and so we have embraced a supine empiricism. Yet this, too, viewed historically, has its rationale. The skeptic is the man with a past and for that reason can move into an intense and vivid present, troubled, bereft of function, but tenacious of the process by which the present becomes his own. Who will trust tomorrow who has no trust in the past? Those who seize only the day suspect the morrow—*quam minimum credulo postero*. And so the skeptic will save his present in the City of God or in the benevolent reason of the Demiurge. The skeptical mistrust is the introduction to metaphysics. After all, it is asking a great deal of man who deals in philosphy that he expose the deplorable errors of great men or vouch for their trustworthiness in the unsullied lucidity of his own learning. Still, what is one to do? What can one do apart from the historical? It is the skeptic, and he alone, who has revealed our stake in the actual and so in the historical. The timeless, when it is not a metaphysic, reveals the man without a past. He who speaks from a historical past speaks ideally, and speaks for himself, extending the continuum of what has been done. To leave ourselves out of the story is to discard deeds as revelatory in the interests of an innocence which no person can then claim as his own. Innocent knowledge waits upon the disinterested act.

Primitive societies, not yet in history, exhibit no problematic past. Although not without stories of origin they view their originating forces as in the same psychic world as the present. Primitivism lends itself to the description of anthropology rather than to the reflectiveness of history. It lacks a past described only in thoughtfulness and consequently lacks a self-conscious present as well. The past is then factual, the antecedents of present facts. The present is not identified as a moment in constitutional revision. In primitivism man is described as he happens to be rather than as he has become for reasons which only he can give. He may seem ignorant and mistaken, but not unnatural, and not perverted from nature by the intrusion of his own deliberate thought. He is not yet a skeptic. Time is not yet out of joint even though rain be scarce and sickness epidemic. There he is, a man without benefit of man, and without the hazard of man. He and his own thoughts do not threaten his natural beliefs. Whatever ensues upon primitivism runs the risk of seeming pretentious. Nature begins to be defined in the way we think, and most securely itself in so far as accident is penetrated by order and comprehended through ideal form. Early philosophers show this concern in the nature of things. Anaximander wrote on nature as did Heracleitus, Xenophanes, Empedocles, and Anaxagoras. While not at all psychological, nature was becoming ideal. Anaxagoras thought that "what appears is a vision of the unseen." In Lampascus where he died after his expulsion from Athens the citizens erected in his memory an altar to Mind and Truth.

Primitivism shows experience not in charge of itself, and so not yet artificial. This does not suggest that pre-history is "realistic" in the modern sense, as if there were a difference between the world as experienced and as it was in itself. Such a distinction is highly sophisticated and occurs after disillusionments and conflicts have occasioned mistrust. Theories of the real mark the loss of naive immediacy. There is no innocent thought once thought has been identified. Any mistake has an introvertive quality and it always requires the past tense. It appears, then, that all criticism and all philosophy are open to the charge of pretentiousness. Back-to-nature movements of all sorts exhibit essays in the evasion of formality, whether in dress, address, or economics. They show that man finds it difficult to live with himself, with his own discoveries about himself. No doubt formality grows rigid, but it does so because it forgets its genesis and purports to be timeless. "Fashion," says Emerson, "is virtue gone to seed; it is a kind of posthumous honor . . . it is a hall of the Past." And so wherever one meets thought one meets man in charge of himself, and this seems pretentious. Quite subtle minds desire a reversion to primitivism, not of course in practical matters, but in accounts of nature and of ourselves. It is for this reason that skepticism has lost influence and its idealized sequels have seemed no better than pretentious nonsense, not "literally" true, not "verifiable" in some region, or in some procedure, where we submit to an absolute accident. One has to take these protestations seriously, for it is beyond question that "matter" makes no sense to Berkeley, or "necessary connections" to Hume.

On the other hand, nobody can plausibly recommend himself in so far as he protests impotence of thought. If there be no disputing about taste it is because taste is taken to be outside criticism. It is innocent, one is to be under no judgment because of it. Innocence of mind, when cognitive, is in the same case. But, then, the skeptic, too, is an innocent man in so far as his condition reflects no device for the satisfaction of a prior aim. He merely discovers himself and may not like what he finds. If he has visions they are characteristically unflattering to his finitude and work, indeed, to the peril of finite importance.

Skepticism and its sequel exist in intensities of self-con-

sciousness. The timeless is not intense apart from the moment which invokes it for its order and fulfillment. Whatever is intense passes away. It is unstable. It can result in the
fixed tensions of psychic disease, or in the absorption of ec-
stacies which end with the dinner bell or the begging bowl.
Love and war, in one form or another, make for powerful
intensities, but in so far as they result in deeds they create
new situations and enforce unexpected attentions. It is only
intensity passing into action which regenerates itself in the
continuum of a productive novelty. Action is certified in
this continuum. The escape from time, wherever it occurs,
and in whatever form, lays an indictment on the actual
moment which suggested it, but on a moment, a momen-
tum, without which the escape lacks occasion. History as a
dimension of experience is the discovery of those concerns
which exist only in their prolongation, enlisting original
intensities in the sustainment of their destined revisions. It
is history, not truth, which cherishes the past. History is
piety. But in meeting and producing the future it also generates a past. The past is the form of intensities which, to be
preserved, have taken on new formalities. A convenient
test for ahistoric states of mind occurs in the question
"Does this view contemplate its own revision?" Where a
revision rests on accident, on a change of mind not ascribed
to the maintenance of finitude but to the passive modifica-
tions induced by an ahistoric environment, one is not in
history. Time is there not of the essence.

If much, or perhaps too much, is here made of skepticism it is only for the reason that the ahistoric found its
occasion in the suspicion of finitude and finitude its authority in this very impasse. This is the source of the persisting
strength of the ahistoric and of its wide prevalence. Much
current philosophy is a contest over what sort of ahis-
toricity is to find favor. It is felt, and rightly, that if one
wants "truths" one must employ an orientation which is,
for the time being, timeless. One has recourse to weights
and measures, to numbers, to usages which preserve a steadiness as one determines how far, how much, what time,
what guilt, what sense, what validity. In whatever way the

ahistoric is encountered one may observe an essay in holding together a present experience in bonds of organization
purporting to be timeless, i.e., of no date, and so not expressive of finite actuality with its menacing mutability.
Our hopes and our knowledge have seemed to require a
non-temporal steadiness. In our limitation we feel no sufficient warrant for critical dicta. This insufficiency is not,
however, a fact, but an experience of selfhood. Its disclosure is no conscious phenomenon, but a reflective self-
consciousness. The arbitrary or the random disconcerts
only the scrupulous and the responsible, those for whom
the sayer and doer embody the perilous authority of utterances. Communication is social, but it is also solitary in its
risky composure. The assassination does not trammel up
the consequences, nor does any word. Deed and word call
down upon themselves the judgment which their own
order invokes. This core of liability is the skeptical insight.
It is the condition of all deeds, of events which fix the
moment, rescuing the deed from anonymity and making it
one's own.

The age is not notably devoted to the eternal. But in so
far as it is not, it seems also to have lost a basis for reverence
and responsibility. The humanities lack authority, and
those who pursue them speak without seeking justification
in a region which man does not define, a region which
shelters and produces thought and action but is also irrelevant to them in its anonymous impersonality.

11

What Does Art Do?

What makes painter-artists interesting? By common standards they seem a rather low lot. But at the same time they do have passion or intensity. Something about the visual world fascinates them. In some way what is seen becomes sharply focused, but what permits this concentration is obscure. All intensity is in the interest of some general purpose. What is it that is brought to a focus?

A physician also brings facts to a focus. So does a scientist reading a gauge of some sort. The weather map is such a concentration of data. And so it goes.

It seems, further, that painting-art may deal with any visual materials, ships, cabbages, and kings. All one has for sure is this focus-quality. But a focus seems to need a whole world of some sort in order to become a point of concentration. A "symptom" stands out, is declarative and eloquent of a disease, and may have wide implications in physiology, chemistry, diet, habits, psychology, etc. That seems to be the sort of situation which allows a "focus" to occur, and to be sought.

So, one may ask, "what is the painter looking for?" It seems he must be looking for something. There are those who say that one paints just what one sees. But that isn't plausible. A biologist draws what he sees, an amoeba, but it seems not—for that reason—to be "art." A surveyor's sketch is just what is seen, but, again, not art.

So, when one paints, one seems to need to assume that the seeing is directed in some way. It is in that connection that a "focus" gets established, apropos of the concern which directs seeing.

In general, it appears that all visual experience requires direction. There appears to be no seeing-in-general, but only seeing directed by some concern, such as that of the physician, the mariner, the surveyor. That is good psychology. One sees a person looking intently, and one may think "I wonder what he sees in that tree, rock, building, or person."

To say that the gazer finds something interesting is tautologous. Of course he does. But any interest carries one into the question of focus, of relevance to some articulated concern. A hungry man looks at a fowl thinking to eat it, a prospector at a rock, thinking to read the presence of gold or lead or uranium. Interest occurs apropos of some larger concern, and it is that concern which controls the seeing and allows another to say what is being seen.

The painter must see something which makes him want to paint, just as the hungry man sees what makes him want to eat. Somehow, the *only* thing the painter sees is whatever it is that makes him want to paint.

If you ask him why he paints you will probably not get a good answer. Some say it is therapeutic or restful. Others that it shows what is really there, what one really sees. But one really sees food in a fowl just as much as beauty. Anyhow, one finds nothing at all merely by looking where there is no prior concern. The hungry man must eat the fowl, the artist in paint must "paint" the fowl.

What makes one want to paint some visual experience? To paint, not to eat, or make a weather map? Plainly, there is some deep urgency, and one not necessarily dependent on social position, or even on schooling and knowledge of the theoretical world. This seems true about actual painters. Some dunce or mad fellow has to paint. He works, he suffers, he accepts harsh judgments. But he paints. This is striking. We don't wonder that anyone wants to eat the fowl; but why paint the bird?

In all these cases the action taken is incidental to a purpose which in the end is ideal. Even eating is done to sustain "life," a most imaginative concept. I will assume this principle. The prospector examines a rock to become rich. The physician makes one well. The plumber stops a leak, and allows domestic practice to continue. All that seems to me quite ideal or imaginative. The painter will be doing the same sort of thing.

In all cases there is a focus upon the object or situation, no more for the painter than for the others. And it is always a focus with a context. Nobody sees the "object" just as object. That is a sensible statement in metaphysics, but not in any context which leads to one sort of action.

I suggest that the painter is engaged in some attempt to establish the visual as object in principle. The physician is already dealing with the region of objects. So is the draftsman. The painter is like the physicist, trying to set up objects as a region, as an order, getting away from vagueness and confusion. In a sense, the physicist is not trying to tell the truth *about* objects; he gives objective status to his confused experience, setting up nature itself. He is not trying to eradicate error either. He is generalizing conditions for making truths and errors possible.

The aesthetic seems, then, somewhat abstractly, to be one of the modes of securing objectivity in principle. That is its "purity." That is the reason why, like physics, it can become a passion.

Objectivity is the other side of selfhood. Only in objectivity is the self real to itself, self-maintaining. This, again, is a general, but well-known, rule.

Another step and assumption: No mode of objectivity occurs in isolation. It occurs because there are other modes of objectivity. Physics illustrates mathematics, and physics nourishes mathematics. Psychology needs logic, and vice versa. It needs history and vice versa. I say this, so as to exclude any attempt to leave painting-art in a vacuum, independent of all other modes of objectivity, and vice versa. Whatever sort of objectivity the painter seeks will be a function of other sorts which he assumes. So with all pure enterprises.

Objectivity depends on artifacts, on "language." Without signs and symbols nature is indistinguishable from the stream of consciousness.

The concern of all passion is the creation of artifacts. Plato saw this in speaking of the generation of beauty. Passion is the demand for objectivity in principle, and is itself wholly inward. The wholly outward is the dialectical opposite of the wholly inward. Passion is the generative source of the non-subjective, the insistence upon having a world.

I think that the difficulty of treating the artist as one who creates a *world* derives from the apparent fact that art—in this case painting—has neither a form nor a content of its own. We can say of mathematics that it deals in the order of quantity, of physics that it explores the order or the form of matter and energy. In this way mathematics and physics project a world, orderly, intelligible, and infinite. But there seems no analogous contribution to nature made by art. It seems to add no new essence, no new mode of intellectual order. Physics and math, although highly intellectual, or theoretical, or ideal, define a region which is not subjective. There one does not think as one pleases, but all is under law and restraint. To suggest a simple example: in claiming that every event has a cause one offers a test for illusion. If one believes the door bell rang, and finds no one on the porch one reasons that one must have been mistaken in supposing that the bell sounded. The bell does not ring without a cause, and there was none. I say this in order to illustrate the claim that science projects a world, and likewise provides a test for appearance and subjectivity.

But nature seems to get along very well without painter-artists. No property of that non-psychological region is determined by a painter. We do not set our watches or run up weather-flags, or determine the location of the magnetic pole by means of any work in an art gallery. Painters have usually been poorly educated in such matters. Paintings propose no errors in our conception of nature. Physics does.

Of course, painters may discover color qualities of objects which have escaped notice. But that is no great matter.

A gardener discovers colors in fruits, vegetables, and flowers which likewise escape the casual observer. Anyone who deals with objects in some special way must learn the qualitative signs which control his operations. The discovery by some painter that snow, closely attended to, exhibited many tints and shades was given such exultant publicity as to leave one inert with amazement.

But even though we owed to painters our knowledge of the visual properties of natural objects (and, in the main, we do not) it would not be through painting that the region of objects had been established. Painting is not a test for any matter of fact, and so not for any illusion. Painting seems not to establish the region of objects in principle.

If not, then it is merely subjective as much without relation to nature as to the order of personality. The mission of all passionate pursuits is to escape from privacy and to establish objective and public reality. Passion is self-defining and nature-defining. Passion is not for "self-expression"; it is for self-establishment where the relinquishment of the passion is a collapse into nonentity. Passion is the energy which moves from nonentity into reality of both self and nature. All reform, and all scientific knowledge, illustrate this unwillingness of the creative mind to fall back into oblivion. Nor is this petty egotism. It is not petty to sustain those endeavors which are disciplinary and perhaps even fatal. For it is in this discipline that one becomes impersonal, objective, and effective.

The mystery of the painting is that it adds no new defining essence to nature, or even to personality. But this suggests that painting, and all art, has another function to perform. It is the function of memorializing or embodying such essences of nature and personality as get defined in the *non-aesthetic forms* of man and nature.

Art has no story of its own to tell, whether about man or nature. It tells no tales which are aesthetic. What it does is to embody in symbols other modes of order. For example, the Lincoln Memorial adds no new fact to the known life, career, or character of Abraham Lincoln. It does not tell what words he spoke, and some of these words are, in fact, inscribed on the wall of the chamber, appearing merely as words. But the memorial notes that the man Lincoln lived. It is a present evidence of his own contribution to the formal order of the state. Without the symbol, whether it be this memorial, or Lowell's poem, or E. A. Robinson's, there is no evidence that anyone had noted the contribution of Lincoln to our understanding of the essence of man. In those notations Lincoln becomes effective.

Art, in all its aspects, has for content the non-aesthetic forms of reality. Religion, as a defining trait of human nature, its concern with destiny, has always secured actual effectiveness through art. Art is an "existential," not an "essential" phase of reality. No orderly mode of thought or action escapes the need of aesthetic symbolization. It is not enough to pray; one must show that one knows that one prays, thereby giving objective status to prayer and all its idealized concomitants. It is not enough to have a society; one must be brought to arrest by the statement of that essence in the actual symbol which makes a nation self-conscious. So, there is a flag, an anthem, many a poem, story, painting, bust, and edifice. It is not enough to have medical science, or trade, or an orderly house; it is necessary that these essences be asserted as the reality of nature and personality. To do that is the function of art.

As a corollary, it follows that no art is concerned with either appearances or facts. A great deal of aesthetic theory flounders in the morass of appearance. The painter, for example, is said to put down what he "sees," or perhaps what he "feels," or "thinks." All that is entirely formless. What the artist notes, memorializes, and converts into force is the self-consciousness of non-aesthetic modes of order. The rapport of mother and child is not aesthetic, but it is a powerful element in the controlled personality. This the artist shows. A country graveyard is a utility or a sign of religious concern, and so can be treated by a poet, without whom we do not "realize" the graveyard, although he adds no new item of content whatever to its area. Nor does the poet add to its meaning. He does not add, he *proclaims*. That proclamation is the actuality of the graveyard as an item in our self-consciousness. And that is our sole reality as persons.

There is art because without art, including the painting-art, there is no way of asserting and proclaiming the relation of non-aesthetic modes of order to the will. The order of man and nature must be not merely understood or even acted out habitually; it must be identified explicitly, and held before us for contemplation. No essential mode of order attains existence until it is so embodied in the symbol. Then, as a mode of order, it enters into will. Art is the reminder of every attained mode of organization to which man is committed, and through which he defines himself. Consequently it is emotionally moving. Its emotion is not the primary violence of instinct, but the much more profound feeling with which we contemplate the structural and organized truth.

These considerations also set the limits of art. Clearly it contributes nothing to our knowledge of essences, whether in nature or in man. It is not physics or psychology. Nor does it contribute directly to history, the process by which man revises his basic forms of order, redefining himself and his world in their fundamental modes of order and control. Nor is it philosophy, the general theory of all criticism. Art is not everything. It is not the same as "culture." But it is necessary as the record of man's realization of such modes of order and control as the non-aesthetic interests have created.

Like all enterprises, art has a history, i.e., a career in the fuller grasp of its own meaning. There is no more reason to suppose that every person who tries rhymes or puts paint on walls is aware of the limiting controls of his work than there is in assuming that all efforts at curing disease realize the intent of medical science. The history of art has two dimensions, and faces two questions. One must ask of an artifact (1) is it art and (2) is it good. A great many things belong to "art" which fall short of fulfilling its intent. An obelisk is a work of art, but a primitive and shady one, just as an incantation is "medicine" but rather incomplete in its grasp of its problem.

At any rate, there is reason to avoid identifying a work of art through such alleged marks as "emotion," imagination, proportion, mass, pleasure, or interest. And one should, of course, avoid expressions purporting to claim that the artist sees what is "really" there. He doesn't, and even if he did the result could not possibly be of aesthetic interest. He deals with existence, not with essence. The question, "what is art?" can be answered by indicating how the aesthetic symbol gives actuality in will, and force in contemplation to all non-aesthetic modes of order. Art can disclose only what is endowed with a prior discipline and imagination. It asserts and proclaims the modes of imaginative and ordered infinity of the non-aesthetic aspects of experience.

This saves art from triviality and from that quite nasty flavor of the esoteric. Art is not, and never has been, esoteric. It has always been a domestic staple. Francis Bacon had something to say about "elegant learning." The reason for the present chaos in art, and in art criticism, derives from our contemporary positivism, i.e., from our current repudiation of non-aesthetic form and authority. Inevitably, the artist flails around in the darkness of his sensations and frustrations and becomes anarchic and incredibly obscure. But where the modern artist has seized upon some objective validity, upon some mode of social and scientific order, he has steadied down to new modes of eloquence and revelation. But such firm eloquence is rare. Once it was common. As the new world of humanism takes shape we may expect art to proclaim its existence, and so make it a self-conscious force.

12

A Meditation on a Painting

I wish to find out what leads me to call this painting by Giotto a work of art. It is a picture of St. Joachim and St. Anne at the Golden Gate in the city of Jerusalem. These two were the parents of Mary, the mother of Jesus. I learn that the picture is found in a chapel in an Italian city. I believe also that it is regarded as elevating the feeling of those who came to the chapel to see parts of the story of Jesus on the walls. Some cannot read; pictures tell them what they could not otherwise discover.

I know, too, that not any sort of picture is found in this chapel. There are only pictures concerning the Christian religion. I have read that many pagan works of art were destroyed by Christian enthusiasts. There is here no representation of Diana of Ephesus, or of Venus of Cyprus. Some works of art seem carefully omitted. The chapel is no museum. One may go to a museum to scoff; one enters the chapel to pray.

I have read too that the Virgin exerted very great power. While this picture was being painted on the wall vast churches were being erected in her honor. I think what a tremendous force she exerted. I remember how Henry Adams regards her as the builder of great religious monuments.

She is worth commemorating, being the mother of

Jesus, and herself born without original sin, a unique status. She is part of the immense plan of God for man's salvation and for his own revelation of human nature. I do not wonder that pictures and buildings should call her to mind. Men, I think, must live by faith and glory. She is part of such a glorious and saving plan.

I look at the picture more closely. It is a simple picture and not a very well drawn one. The gate especially seems unlikely in its construction. I have seen gates, and they are a good deal more formidable than this one. But that does not matter. It is not the gate as an object that draws attention. It is the figures and their common rapport. I find my attention moving toward the two central figures. It is these which center the composition. The picture, I see, *is* a composition. It has composure. There are not two pictures within this frame, but only one. The artist, I think, has known how to secure this unity. It is like an arrow in a bow; all the energy of the body focused on one point, making it powerful. I do not know precisely how the artist contrives such a result. No doubt he has learned how to use colors, tints, shades, lines, the gaze and motion of people, to some focal purpose. I can see that much is omitted from the picture: other people, plants, animals, or buildings which would arouse one's curiosity only to distract attention. It must take much special skill and much study to learn precise speech in color, as in words. Such small changes can make such great obscurity or clarity.

I find the picture elevating. It governs my thought. It brings me into touch with so many of my fellow men who lived and died, one might say, with this picture before them, It has a meaning for me. It does not mean any merely human experience, but the elevation of experience to a part of the divine reality. Many children have been born, many parents made glad. But to most this is no more than a human joy, and may be turned to tears. But *this* joy has another status. It is beyond passing. It is a moment in a great revelation. Time will not eradicate it, but it will stand forever. All this the artist has brought home to me. In him vaguer thought has been given precision. The story becomes his creation, for no story can move one until it is told.

II

But on leaving the chapel I find myself beset with most disturbing thoughts. For I am not one to go to this chapel to pray in the full faith of the Christian believer. Is the artist a seducer of thought? And are there not other artists, the great ones of antiquity, or of the Orient, who have moved men in other ways? Perhaps Plato is right; perhaps artists are betrayers of rigorous self-control.

But an experiment occurs to me. I will turn my copy of the picture upside down. By so doing I will remove every temptation to see objects, and so I will escape those religious feelings which had taken possession of me. I will not be their slave. I will not allow myself to identify the figures in the picture. The stone walls of the gate will no longer be walls.

It seems to me now that my experiment will carry me to many strange results. But I must press on and not be held back because they are strange. Perhaps new understanding will illuminate me and save me from the narrowness of thought and feeling which my own very small experience imposes upon me when I see persons or objects.

I see colors, now. They are not composed into objects. They are not arranged for my intellect so as to reveal objects. That is not their unity, now that the picture is upside down. The color which once served to reveal posture, expression, or object now serves no such purpose. The areas free from objects, and only extending the scene, the better to indicate center and focus, are now no longer such free areas. The skillful use of lines to cause concentration of attention upon the supposedly important figures now concentrate no more since nothing more is revealed in one place than in another. Joachim and Anne have vanished; only a colored area remains. Now of course, I do not see new figures, or new objects. I have seen pictures which had the amusing property of showing a face or object even when turned upside down; but such tricks would spoil the experiment. It would merely mock my experiment were I to find a second set of objects, or any new arrangement of objects, when my purpose is to avoid seeing any object whatsoever.

I see only colors. They are so grouped as to show areas relatively different or relatively alike. I may say, I think, that I see lines, but not the lines which limit an object. The lines float in space, the eye can follow a succession of colors, and that is now a line. There are, in fact, many such lines, but they bound no objects. The picture has become bewildering.

But at this point I will recollect myself. What, after all, did I expect but such a meaningless and unmoving variety? Was I not avoiding unity? I had previously found it in objects, attitudes, feelings, and meaning. I must not now complain if I am at a loss to discover it.

But a thought occurs to me. May not the unity be found in color itself? I see the color. My eye moves. Color and motion; may not these suggest composition? May there not be a unity here? Is there form in color and motion?

That would appear the place to consider. I reflect that if there were form in color it would not be another color. I see clearly that form has an intellectual flavor. Form is not for the eye. Nor, I consider, does motion in itself have form. The eye can move over the entire surface up, down, across. What will arrest these shifting colors? I see very well that the inverted picture offers here and there a line to follow. But I do not know which way to follow it. Nor can I tell. I become lost in these data; they have no shape. They do not compel me. It is true I like some of the colors, and this smoother line arouses no dislike as does that vague and irregular one. But I reflect that it is to avoid such sentiments that I turned the picture.

Yet somehow I know that a work of art should be self-sufficient. It should not send me abroad, but bring me to rest in itself. Was it to avoid this instrumental status that I turned the picture? I believe so. And yet I find that a patch of colors has no rest. It has no rest because it contains no motion. It is chaos, holding neither motion nor rest. The rest of a whole is self-contained motion.

I feel sure of the need of this self-containment. But how I will find it I must leave for another meditation. I know only that I find no form in quality. I know that wiser men than I have insisted on quality alone. I know that *there* lies the ever recurring denial of order. I must see where order can be found. This will be an arduous task, but I must undertake it or end in losing my picture.

13

The Scholar as Man of the World

Education makes us men of the world. It sets before us an ordered totality so that knowledge and action, which are finite and particular, may have a setting in an infinity. In this way it idealizes the immediate situation. The educated man is a man of the world because in a literal sense he perceives and inhabits a world. He stands in a totality illuminated by his thought, and he endeavors to make his thought the vehicle of an endless perspective. To acquire such orientation is the chief motive for advanced study. The search for it explains the excitement and also the desperation of controlled inquiry.

All men possess some perspective, all live in some world, more or less orderly or confused, more or less dark and incoherent, but never wholly formless or inarticulate. But in the scholar the articulate world has become a deliberate quest and an acknowledged need. Such a world cannot be altogether inherited, but must be won afresh by every student, if only that he may the more surely possess it as his own. The scholar must have the courage and the persistence to repossess his heritage and, if possible, to go beyond it.

I propose that we now consider this adventure in some of its data, and in its general implications for the life of a free society. For it is not altogether easy to feel oneself a scholar in the contemporary world. Perhaps it has never been easy, because deliberate study, particularly when formal, must to some extent alienate the inquiring mind from standard habits and values. Study brings into question the very stability which surrounds it and which makes it possible. The questioning mind is always to some extent set apart because it sets itself apart. The fraternity of scholarship is based on respect for this risky independence and for all who accept its burdens and obligations.

In this process the student is himself liable to be disturbed in his composure and simple integrity. He may not always receive an answer to his questions, and no answer may be known to teachers, or even discoverable in books. He is on his own, and that is certain to be at times uncomfortable, even though it be also fascinating and glorious. Questions may seem strange even to one's scholarly associates because the motives of questions may be obscure or novel, not well understood by the student himself. Yet in this willingness to stand on one's own ground, cost what it may, is a principal reason for the attraction which the scholar exerts upon others. There is a boldness about it which wins some acknowledgment and sometimes the vague envy of more acquiescent minds. There can be no scholarship where learning is wholly a matter of instruction, as if all the questions had been anticipated, and all the answers worked out in advance. Training conveys no sense of magic, creates nothing new, brings no revision of outlook, and earns no prestige.

In a democracy we need especially to guard against the temper which can so readily reduce all men to mediocrity of spirit. In the end, the free society must be based on respect, and not on equality of consumer's goods. Equal spirits are mysterious to each other and for that reason enticing and authoritative. There can be no urge to community where there is no division, nor where the meaning of the division is not found in the attraction of self-contained inquiry. The society of scholars is necessary in all free association and in it we are redeemed from seeking each other out only for benefits or for practical advantage.

Turning from these large and eventual considerations let

us observe some of the simpler phenomena of educational growth, and the difficulties which attend them. I would like, if I could, to bring these reflections to the conclusion that all education must idealize the actual. That seems to me to be what is open to us to do in our time. We are not likely to feel that we can actualize the ideal. We are not sure what the ideal may be, nor, in any abstract formulation of it, is there likely to be agreement. But we may, I suggest, find in the process of growth some intimations of the form of our world and of the human spirit. For at the close of college studies one needs to capture that morale which gives authenticity to what has been done and assurance to its sequel.

The origins of education are simple because they are natural and spontaneous. This freshness can wither, but, in the end, it must be recaptured. Indeed, its loss is unavoidable, and its return dubious. But it is a quality which may not be forsaken unless education is to result in drabness and in the paralysis of energies.

To the child, experience opens as an absorbing immediacy. There it seeks and finds a present mastery. Failures and frustrations more than balance out in the day's transactions and each day awakens innocent ambitions. Walking, speaking, manipulating bring delightful conquests over circumstances, and a gratified sparkle to the eye of the complacent and conscienceless hero. He lords it over the immediate foreground and is content with his ability to bring it under control. In a systematic sense he has no world at all, and no soul which stands opposed to his environment.

It would, however, be a mistake to overlook the artificiality of the circumstances within which this spontaneity operates. For the child all is natural and unforced, but for the parent its activities are known to require a carefully guarded setting. The most natural development is also the most artificial. The child finds great scope in a crib, a pen, or in a room. A sandbox of generous proportions offers a scene of enormous possibilities to the imagination and to practical exploits. Yet all this has been provided, and that fact seems sufficient to refute extreme claims for back-to-nature theories of education. What is called "progressive education" translates these opportunities to the school, so-liciting natural impulses in the mastery of objects and social situations. It is often thought wise to allow all correction to spring from the direct failures of these lively engagements, so that all external, and perhaps all arbitrary, rebuff may be avoided.

There can probably be no disqualifying doubt that this cult of the spontaneous has marked a prime advance in educational practice. There used to be too much rote learning, and too much birching. Old cuts of school rooms in books on the history of education show the schoolmaster armed with stick and rods. It seems likely that, as the fund of knowledge has grown larger, and as this accumulation has been clearly seen to be the deposit of our own free efforts, the propriety, and even the need, of furnishing to every child the flavor of naturally acquired knowledge has become inarguable. To do otherwise would be to falsify the heritage into which he must eventually enter, and which he must administer in the same spirit which produced it. "Every oracle," says Emerson, "must be interpreted by the same spirit that gave it forth."

But spontaneity must come to an end, at least in this original and uncritical form. Perpetual security is beyond our power to provide, however well disposed some might feel themselves to be, and however ready to contain the natural man. A program for such containment is offered by Aldous Huxley in *Brave New World*. It may strike one as curious that adults who must manage the risky enterprises of an open society should be content, and even eager, to permit these protected origins to education and to extend them into adolescence and beyond. Against this progres-sivism one might bring the charge of a fostered sense of unreality which will be bound to cause trouble, as restric-tions and obligations curb uncriticized impulses. There may even ensue psychical conflicts as the more arbitrary and theoretical factors of nature and society make them-selves felt and can be no longer ignored or evaded. In rec-ognizing this limitation on the spontaneous we need not, however, forget that it is an inevitable first stage. The scholar, too, must possess some immunity to the invasion of practical demands if he is to find time to read a book and to allow himself to become arrested in the muddles of thoughtfulness. Education entails this surplus of means if there is to be time for stories and theoretical inquiry, for ceremony, and for choice among activities.

That there exists a surplus of means is a property of the environment which gradually dawns on the growing child. This revelation is of great importance, for it discloses that one is the beneficiary of a type of control with which one is not yet familiar. There comes at last the perception that one's innocent waywardness is itself the sign and evidence of a more deliberate order than spontaneity could itself generate or maintain. Our first world does not exceed our consciousness, and it comes into new existence with every healthy morning. Our second world embraces and includes the days, because it is the necessary condition of their recurrence. The first suggestions of the impersonal are borne upon the perception of this powerful control which harbors leisure and permits adventure. There is the inception of wonder that goes beyond curiosity, and the summons to a control which exceeds psychological impulsiveness.

The revelation of this new order appears most sharply as constraint. This factor in education has seemed to many as undesirable or even as arbitrary and tyrannous. But I believe that this is not so. Constraint in its simplest, but also in its systematic meaning, is the price of the spontaneous. It appears as the need of routine, as drill, and as habit. It has the flavor of things needing to be done whether one wishes to do them or not. Chores must be performed, some facts or practices learned by heart, even when one's heart is not in them. Property must be kept in order. All this must be attended to, however alien it may appear to direct interest. Such authority may loom as punishment, the actual enforcement of the priority of environment over impulse. In these disclosures and encounters there occur the first truly systematic compulsions. And, of course it is at this point that educators themselves are likely to fall out with each other, suspecting a shiftless anarchy on the one side, or a dogmatic arbitrariness on the other.

I would not propose to defend the propriety of constraint by treating it as if it might be avoided, but for good reasons must be imposed. To defend it on such grounds suggests an ulterior motive, such, for example, that it builds character, or is good for the soul, or that it must be accepted eventually, so why not now. Such a line of interpretation would seem to me ill-advised. It assumes a managerial wisdom, perhaps even an ultimate wisdom, on the part of adults about which they themselves may differ, and which the child may itself come to challenge and perhaps repudiate.

I would rather propose to understand restraint as "existential learning" and as the occasion of control over an actual but limited and precarious order. The defect of spontaneity, and its consequences when made absolute, lies in its inability to identify and control its own conditions. It is this obliviousness which we feel, perhaps vaguely, to be the shortcoming of some versions of progressive education. In the encouragement of subjectivity it leaves the established world a mystery, never quite revealed in its necessity and authority, and so in the end, not in its majesty and infinity. Spontaneity is robbed of its own sweetness and of its residual power when it becomes the sole source of control. It eventuates not in equanimity, but in an opacity to the demanding issues in which the conquests of the mind and spirit find their objectification.

Existential learning derives from the mastery of the insistent foreground. It is of that immediacy that we must take charge in principle. It is, indeed, the sole region of control and power. We control only local situations, and not the universe as a whole. But such control has its own enticements. We are not satisfied with spontaneity for a reason that seems to me at once simple and profound. It is that we do not there encounter a systematic antagonist, or any systematic demand. A systematic demand threatens us with an equally systematic frustration, with some vanishment of power unless it be acknowledged and met in its inexorable presence. Whatever any man may say about that inexorable presence is the portrait of his philosophy, and so of the outlines of his mind and of his world. But by acknowledging it, and only so, can one become a man of the world. We need to ally ourselves with the antagonist if experience is not to remain merely playful and subjective and so in the end, trivial and without dignity. If experience and education are to become means of asserting *our* power they must identify themselves with *objective* power. And to be clearly identified, every power must loom as a threat when ignored.

It is for this reason that the child is not altogether disconcerted when demands are made upon it. In such conformity it discovers a control no less desirable than the fruits of its own natural impulsiveness. Even punishment, when it clearly represents the unapologetic attempt to maintain local control, and is so perceived, breeds no lasting resentment. On the contrary, it suggests rather the security without which activity has no limits and no guard. And so education moves into the control of the conditions of security. Existential knowledge, born of restraint, furnishes the sole avenue to such actual, if limited, power as we possess, or can come to possess.

There can be no greater deception in education than that of leading anyone to believe that he can get what he wants, or that by doing what he wants he can acquire the power of knowledge. All pretension to knowledge rests in the end on the claim that one has grappled with a systematic and objective antagonist. If one wrestles it must be with an angel, in order to win his secrets. In our time knowledge has lost some of its dignity by being presented as nothing more than a tool or means for meeting an environment to which we are to become adjusted. Such a view breaks our alliance with the compulsory. It leaves nature and society alien to our wills as we seek for a subjectivity which we know to be doomed. In the child's experience of order, and of his need for it, there appear in simple form both an unarguable demand and an alliance with it.

These seem to me the initial and true sources of an education which can authorize scholarship. The scholar is not indulging his caprice in ways more elaborate or subtle than those of the engrossed child. Nor is he attempting by his great wit to steal a march on less gifted, or less fortunate, men in order to seize the means of private satisfaction. He is not the altruist, doing good in the world, transferring to others the subjective satisfactions more properly enjoyed by them than by himself. He is rather the person who has made an alliance with the imperative and actual foreground, accepting its discipline and giving expression to its implications.

Natural science and mathematics illustrate the organization of present and actual situations. They are extensions of immediacy. Without yardsticks, clocks, balances, and similar instruments the order of nature remains undiscovered. It is said that meteorology as weather prediction depended upon Toricelli's discovery of the barometer. The inquirer into nature's ways begins with these modest, but eloquent and powerful, artifacts. All controlled statements are made in terms of their order. It is so also with mathematics, originally a question of counting or of keeping a tally with stones or pebbles, from which we derive the word "calculate." Here we find an articulate finitude. This, I venture to say, is also what one means by an infinity. It is what one means by a "world." The function of scholarship is the discovery and maintenance of such modes of the infinite forms of finite actuality.

Natural science has been scolded at times because it is said to deal with the dead world from which man is excluded. Certainly there are no purposes in test tubes. But there is something very like purpose in measurement when it is viewed as the specification of the local and actual for the sake of clarity and control. The constitutional aspects of objects do not, it is true, serve a particular purpose, but a knowledge of them sets the stage for the execution and formulation of *all* purposes as they may happen to occur. The impersonality of science should not be taken to mean its irrelevance to the local, the particular, or the actual. It consists rather in its comprehensive view of the general condition of all purposes.

In dealing with nature we must, accordingly, beware of proving too much. If nature were only an impersonal object we might leave it alone and go our ways. If it were only matter we might turn to the cultivation of our spirits. The trouble with such arguments is that they overlook the fact that we are in league with our circumstances, and that they can be described only in terms of our own exertions. It is the need of local control that generates our interest in the farthest star cluster and the most recondite constituent of the atom. All these are the implications of an articulate immediacy, nor have they any other bearing on an educational program. The neglect of nature is no triumph of the spirit, but is equivalent to the claim that there is no educational worth in counting one's pennies or in doing the household chores. Of course, one cannot altogether exonerate natural scientists who sometimes give the impression that they are either the servants of psychological impulses or else the contemplators of a region divorced from our self-maintenance. I believe that they are neither, but that they cultivate the formal order which invests the immediate and projects it into an articulate infinity. They are men of the world. They have a world.

Perhaps these suggestions indicate the relation between scholarship and our own energies. It would be strange if what begins in childhood as vigorous activity were to eventuate in placidity and contemplation. The truth seems to be that all scholarship has been created by extremely active men, even when they have recommended the meditative or withdrawn life. We are very apt to be deceived by this substitution of a result for a process. It is true that Plato felt that one did well to become the "spectator of all time and all existence," but it seems hardly plausible to infer from this that one could write a Platonic dialogue if one were to neglect Socrates or Alcibiades, or the turbulent politics of Athens in decay. Aristotle's life of reason concerned with external objects and their timeless forms must somehow be made consistent with his having written a great many books, so intricate and fundamental that Western scholarship still employs his classifications and categories. Professor John Dewey has built a splendid case for the modern world on the claim that until recently scholarship was drowsy with the contemplative ideal. I doubt that Plato was particularly dreamy himself, or that nobody felt the need of power prior to Francis Bacon. What there is of truth in Dewey's claim seems to be rather that the enormous energies necessary to discover and express the order of experience can in the end find no adequate cause until they confess their concern with the particular. It used to be supposed, and it still is in many quarters, that the particular is irrational and that it is to be redeemed only in some inarticulate totality. When that view is taken, the description of discipline as something which is identical with the maintenance of circumstances must, of course, be rejected. What I am here suggesting is that we do not lose a world, but gain one, as we identify our own power with the power of circumstance in its orderly form. The scholar can do nothing about an abstract infinity. There is nothing to be said about it and nothing to be done about it. It provokes no energies and vouches for the propriety of no actual control. The scholar does not dwell in the night in which all cows are black, as Hegel observed.

Perhaps Emerson could serve as an example of a man whose thought expresses the conflict between present actuality and an ideal somewhat remote and contemplative. He says that he stands in the sun and expands like the corn and the melons. Benign, open to every influence, uncontentious, he laid himself open to the illuminations of nature and of history. Yet on the other side he was an independent man, urging us to trust our emotions and to do the day's work. Himself a reformer of sorts, he voiced the issues of the day and paid a personal price for his insurgency and integrity. Although his scale is weighted on the side of the receptive, yet it trembles downward at times under the heaviness of place, time, and circumstances, and the need of action. It seems safe to say that he was a man of the world. "There is one mind common to all individual men," he wrote in his essay on history. And there were the lines:

> There is no great and no small
> To the soul that maketh all,

> And where it cometh all things are,
> And it cometh everywhere.

Our increasing concern with the local and particular may seem to have invaded such security and assurance. At the same time the very achievements of responsible control have tended to give progressive embodiment to our ideals. We have to an unprecedented extent domesticated an orderly world in pursuing the implications of the closer environment. Whatever one may feel about this it can hardly bring an accusation of vagrancy against the scholar. He is a responsible person though he concern himself with such quite human achievements as grammar and logic.

These are the thoughts which have often occurred to me at commencement. For it is a grievous thing to see the young student depart without those convictions upon which his morale depends. He must see himself authenticated, not so much by others, as by his own conviction that he has at least descried the outlines of an endless order in his own studies, and that the society of which he is a member expects from him a temper which accords with the pursuit of these disinterested perspectives. The scholar is not a furtive appropriator of superior means, but a free man in the perception of a world which is the form of his endeavors. And who shall say in his fidelity to circumstance no serenity may at last be found? Any actual serenity that is not illusion and abdication occurs in the enjoyment of the strength which can steadily sustain an ordered outlook.

Responsibility in the actual means that time must be taken seriously as a dimension of our own reality. But what we do there has the curious quality of generating a fatality merely because we have acted. There are oriental philosophies which have made much of this fatal entanglement. In the celebrated *Bhagavad Gita* there is posed the problem of how a man can act without taking sides, for in taking sides we are implying that the truth and the good are to be found one way rather than another. To act is to see oneself as limited, and as a trustee for value, especially when the act is warlike, and so destructive of life and of antagonistic values. This is the entanglement with the finite which lures us into the dimension of time. The Oriental doctrine proposes that one would do ill to take that dimension quite seriously. It urges that time and history can bring no actual completion to the intellect, nor to the desires of men. In that dimension we must remain incomplete. Consequently, we should seek a fulfillment apart from all "name and form," apart, that is, from the articulate. No actual moment is ever the auspicious one for the acceptance of circumstance. All circumstance must be treated as if it lacked power to reveal the ideal or could become the occasion for insight and freedom.

However attractive, and it always attracts distressed minds, this disqualification of the articulate and of the temporal has never dominated Western thought. We have always found some value and truth in concern with circumstance. Knowing that inquiry is limitless, we persist in it. Although every proof rests on hypothesis, yet we go on with our syllogisms and experiments. Every institution generates problems out of its very excellences. We have not disavowed consequences in principle. On the contrary, we have tended to feel that our thought can be tested for truth or error only as consequences are identified and observed. We have established societies, and now at last free societies, which deliberately propose to make change possible in an endless reinterpretation of the conditions of freedom. We see the ahistoric as the static, and so, in terms of practice, as the despotic. For only despotism can bring the career of experience to an end.

There is growth and education only in so far as our words and deeds have consequences. In a play or novel plot is the return upon an agent of his own action, to his illumination and instruction. What one *is* has no way of being revealed other than through the outcome of what one does. To learn we must bring something to pass, speak a sentence which leads to confusion or to clarity, do an act which enlarges or confounds our powers. But if that be the meaning of education then history is the record of that learning in its constitutional aspects. Psychology too is concerned with learning, but with skills and habits rather than with that revision of outlook which concerns history.

As a coercive, and, hence, as a disciplinary, region of experience history has the peculiar quality of depending entirely on our own willingness to act. It is not an area passively perceived, and no one, so far as I know, has been satisfied to leave us out of the picture entirely. It is a great power, and a region of fate, which we deliberately espouse as the inclusive school of experience.

I submit that the scholar must espouse it, just as firmly as he allies himself with nature in the physical sciences. Indeed, science itself has a history, a record not only of accumulation, but of basic revisions in controlling concepts and procedures. None of that could have come to pass were men to resign themselves from the actual. To disavow time is to reject learning. It is to reject criticism, whether in comedy or tragedy, or in logic, or in the constitutional law of the state.

The importance of consequence to criticism has been stressed by the school of moralists called utilitarians, and also by the pragmatists. The utilitarians were earnest men, social reformers, who had tired of formal ethics. They proposed that the moral value of an act be determined by its results. Good intentions they considered insufficient, not only because that left the act quite private, but because no open way of judging it seemed possible. What is here proposed, however, is not utilitarianism but rather the need of commitment to those formal processes which generate consequences. History is such a process. It is the story of the consequences of our commitments. For that reason it is a region of ultimate risk. It is this property of history which gives it both fascination and terror. It is fascinating because it necessitates abandonment. It is terrifying because it entails the treatment of some actual program as the absolute necessity of the moment. On the whole I would say that men are modest, and more given to mistrusting themselves than to pretensions to perfection. But in history they say that we can "do no other." Or they say that we must "do the right as God gives us to see the right." I think that the force of these statements needs no elaboration. They indicate what is meant by our inability to escape history. We cannot escape commanding our circumstances. It seems to mean that. We cannot escape attempting to clothe finitude in the forms of criticism whether in physics or in politics.

All this may seem a long way from the spontaneous child and its slow discovery of the controlled environment which guards his fresh impulsiveness. It is indeed a long way, and yet, I hope, a continuous and unbroken way. All that we can do in education, in so far as our aim is scholarship, is to enlarge that environment. It is our rude antagonist, but it is also our ally. As nature and as history it appears as fate. One gets a clue to these fateful dimensions when one finds what one tries systematically to elude or circumvent. But the scholar has learned that it is only a fateful power which is also his own. He learns that he must immerse in the destructive element and that he will drown if he tries to climb out of that vast sea.

You may perhaps think that all this is a bit grandiose, a lot of high-flying. Well, a child is surely down to earth, and I have been doing no more than sketch what some child encounters in his search for knowledge and command. I fear we are stuck with this story, or another one very much like it. For my part, I cannot bear easily seeing young men leave college enervated in their morale or treating the areas of order as if they were incidental to the meaning of their own prospects of power and discipline. Education should be practical, one is told, and with this one must agree. But what can it be that relates scholarship to the will of man if not its literal embodiment of his thoughtful destiny? I do not feel that science and history have detracted from the authority of the spirit. Quite the other way, it seems to me that there the spirit finds its sole articulate reality and the will its sole manageable commitment. The scholar can deal only in the fateful, but he overcomes fate by identifying himself with its laws. There seems to me quite enough romance in this to satisfy anyone. What more is there than to stand in the presence of that order, at once disciplinary and infinite, through which any world can get defined?

The perception that the immediate is the locus of law is suggested by Paul in the epistle to the Romans. There Paul with his characteristic intensity wishes to avoid a life that is forever under the law and never in itself the generator of law. That is a bold idea indeed. But to Paul this self-generated law finds its actuality in charity. In that spirit, he believed, one can act out of oneself and without offense. But charity needs an object. It is not a boost to morale to deny that some object can be the worthy recipient of disinterested regard. We dare not postpone sufficiency and we dare not postpone the law. Otherwise we will "take the cash and let the credit go, nor heed the rumble of a distant drum." I am proposing that the scholar has made his alliance with fate, and that in so doing he restores to discipline the original spontaneity which first appeared as childish impulsiveness. To bring these two ends together has been the object of these remarks. But that this is possible requires the career of education, and even the temporary separation of impulse from discipline. They are united not in desire, but in will. The will is the force that commits us to all the modes of systematic order. That is the reason why the will is free. It does not give us what we want, but it holds us to those endeavors which permit the emergence of law. It is our alliance with law and so with the fateful powers.

At the end it may be suitable to say a word about the role of philosophy. As I see it philosophy is the deliberate endeavor to discover the loci of systematic conflict. It is the essay in maintaining a world that is threatened with dissolution under its own internal stresses. It belongs in education—though you may think me now partisan and unreliable—because nobody understands the appeal of order in principle until it is threatened in principle. There is no doubt about the excitement that students feel when they are first brought to face not an error of fact, but an incoherence in the form of the facts, and so in the report which we make of the facts. Let me illustrate this from some of the preceding ideas.

The philosophy of history is a comparative novelty. In the main our knowledge has had an ahistoric ideal. This appeared originally as theology and later as natural science. Time was not of the essence, and all events in time were treated as illustrations of uniformities in which yesterday and today were indistinguishable. Whether at Hobart or at Williams salt is sodium chloride. Whether at Pisa or at Poona the laws of the pendulum are the same. These uniformities have stood as the desideratum of inquiry. Accordingly it is odd to find serious men treating events in time as if they had some order of their own. And, of course, there are views of history which reduce it to physics or to psychology, when the full truth is known. But there actually exists historical knowledge in which such an ultimate truth is not now the control of history-writing. There one finds cropping up the quite scandalous tendency to treat events as unique, and not, accordingly, to be reduced to a formula. Is there, then, any knowledge of the unique? To say so appears to fly in the face of all logic and orderly procedure.

If you have ever been involved in such a conflict you will know what philosophy is about. There are many examples, and different persons find their world coming apart in different places. Some wonder whether the language of biology and psychology should be translated into the language of physics, or vice versa. Others find trouble in the opposition of determinism and freedom, or in the primacy of the empirical or rational procedures. These are familiar occasions for the onset of philosophy.

Education cannot include philosophy until the student already possesses and values formalized modes of knowledge. It is in terms of such assumed organizations that the philosophic problem arises. One may say that philosophy deals in "organization words," not in "denotation words." In an older style these are called "categories"; in a newer style "presuppositions," or "postulates," or "operational rules."

The present purpose, however, concerns education, and philosophy, if at all, only in so far as it too would help to make us men of the world. To be brief and direct on this relationship, I will say that nobody can evade the confusions which lurk in thought precisely where thought is at its most systematic. No articulate world is without these systematic discontinuities. I will give an example which is of the utmost simplicity.

The original order of experience was in terms of value-control. The answer to the question "Why does it thunder?" is given in terms of the purposes of Zeus or Thor. Such views of order are not superstitious but quite empirical and realistic. This is so because original control is suggested by what one does. One throws a stone directing it at a target. The explanation of that change occurs through purpose, the only sort of control directly apprehended. But it soon developed that objects to be controlled had to have a "nature." One threw a stone, not a piece of wood, or a round stone rather than a flat one. Part, at least, of the event needed to be explained in terms of the properties of the object. Without dependable sequences in nature purpose can neither formulate nor execute itself. But, in consequence, the region of objects, including in the end the human body, takes on the properties of the objective order and enjoins purposive explanation of any event whatsoever. Nature, discovered as the condition of action, now devours its parent. In consequence thought is in conflict with itself. It is not in conflict with the facts, but with its own incoherent modes of interpreting the facts, or, rather, of arriving at them.

Such differences also break out between men, as well as within the individual. When that happens there is likely to be animosity or even warfare. Nor should one be surprised at that. Nobody who intends to be reasonable can lightly abandon the methods by which he himself maintains a measure of control and integrity. And if he acts out his beliefs, establishing schools and societies on their basis, he has laid down a challenge which his declared enemies can hardly ignore.

It is because we are rational that our worlds lack coherence. There is reason in physics and reason in history, but how they relate may be obscure. And so, when the physicist steps into history—and there are recent examples—he may exhibit what many consider unreason. There is reason in psychology and logic, but how psychology could generate the coercions of inference may not be obvious. Yet every man has a stake in all these modes of orderly statement, in all these modes of enlargement and control.

Violence, when it goes beyond the flare-up of a passing passion, is occasioned by these radical conflicts over the controls of our reason, and so of our commitments.

These conflicts are the fatalities of thought and it is the philosophical task to lend itself to these fatalities in order to understand them, and so to reconcile them. The pathos of our deeper antagonisms lies in this fact, that they are always the signs of what we must respect, namely some essay at a rational world. Philosophy is the reason that seeks to comprehend the loci of the breakdown of reason.

Wherever there is conflict there is already some self-control, whether within oneself, or between persons. Philosophy is the attempt to control one's own systematic thought, and to exert control over others in so far as they are in control over themselves. There are other types of control. There are force control, economic control, psychological control, and the control of prestige in its various forms. But all these are irrelevant to philosophy, which can operate only in a mind urged by its own incoherence to re-establish control over itself. In this way it is part of education because it is a factor in the establishment of a world. Just as the child must identify itself with those coercive circumstances which enforce habit, discipline, and formal inquiry, so the more mature individual must identify himself with the menacing powers of division in the very constitution of his thought. In all cases one must immerse oneself in the destructive element. In all cases one's own powers are found in alliance with one or another form of fatality. We must grasp the nettle and not evade circumstance or hope for any insight or power apart from the systematic implications of local control. And those, I believe, will always indicate the presence of an infinity, i.e., a world.

In conclusion, I may say that my object has been simple. It was to reconcile spontaneity and discipline as the two elements in education. Any ordered totality, being articulate, can be sustained only by our efforts. It is indeed equivalent to what one could mean by one's mind. Its maintenance and extension are equivalent to what one could mean by one's will.